Art with Captions
A Museum Lover's Book of Cartoons

Featuring Cartoons From
Barron's
The New Yorker,
Wall Street Journal
& more!

Front Cover illustration: Guy Richards Smit
Back Cover illustration: Hilary Allison
Introduction: Bob Mankoff
Edited By: Darren Kornblut

Dedicated to Jennifer, Bea, Cor,
and all my friends in the museum community

Cartoon Collections, LLC
10 Grand Central, 29th Floor
New York, NY 10017

For cartoon licensing information visit www.cartoonstock.com
Create a custom version of this book at www.cartoonstockgifts.com

First edition published 2024

Item # 49236
ISBN: 978-1-963079-08-1

Introduction

Ah, the world of art, museums, and culture—a veritable treasure trove of inspiration for the cartoonist's pen. It is with great delight and a hint of mischievousness that I welcome you, to this whimsical collection of cartoons that aim to capture the essence of the artistic realm and the captivating world of museums.

As the former Cartoon Editor of *The New Yorker*, I have had the pleasure of sifting through countless cartoons that offer a unique lens into the human experience. With this book, I invite you to embark on a journey where wit and satire intersect with canvases and sculptures, illuminating the humor and idiosyncrasies that pervade the hallowed halls of culture.

Within the pages of this book, you'll encounter a delightful cast of characters, including eccentric artists and bemused onlookers, who navigate the complex landscapes of art and its institutions. They will guide you through a comical exploration of the fickle nature of artistic interpretation, the peculiarities of art connoisseurship, and the humorous clash between tradition and innovation.

Prepare to be regaled with the antics of misplaced masterpieces, where the line between genius and child's play blurs with delightful absurdity. These cartoons will bring a mischievous grin to your face as you witness the art world through a lens of playful irreverence. With each stroke of the cartoonist's pen, you'll find yourself contemplating the very nature of creativity, provoking laughter and contemplation in equal measure.

Bob Mankoff

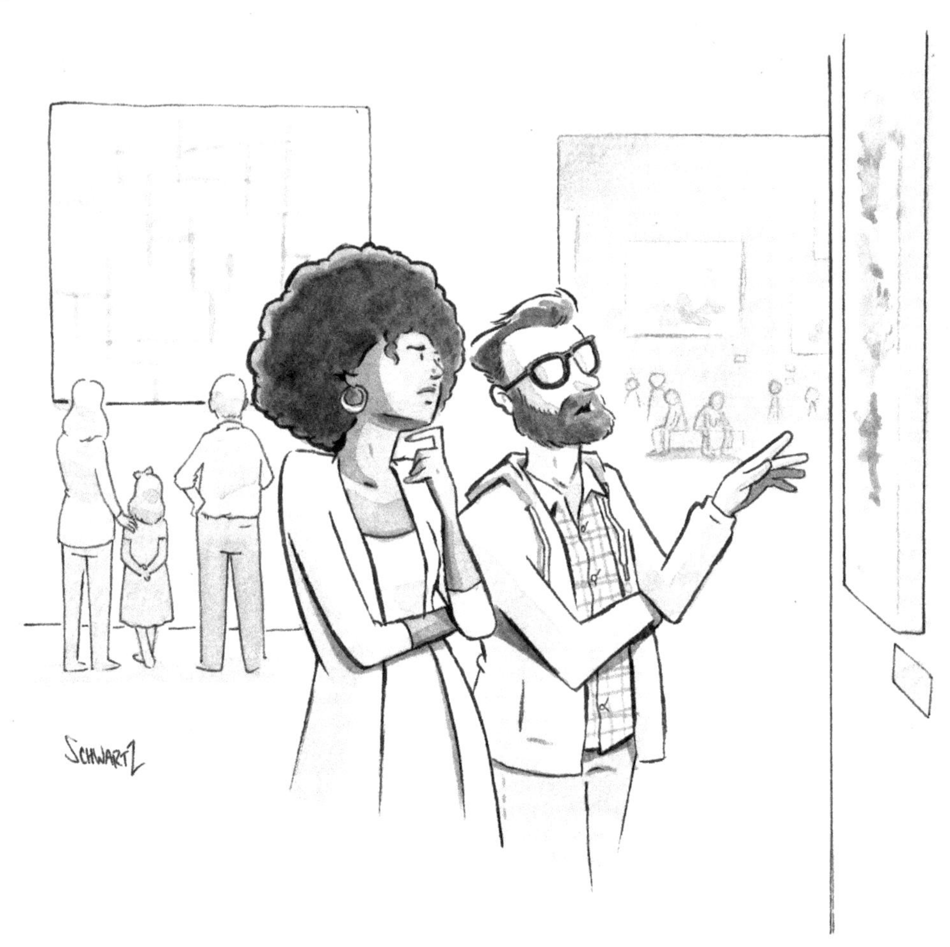

"But is it content?"

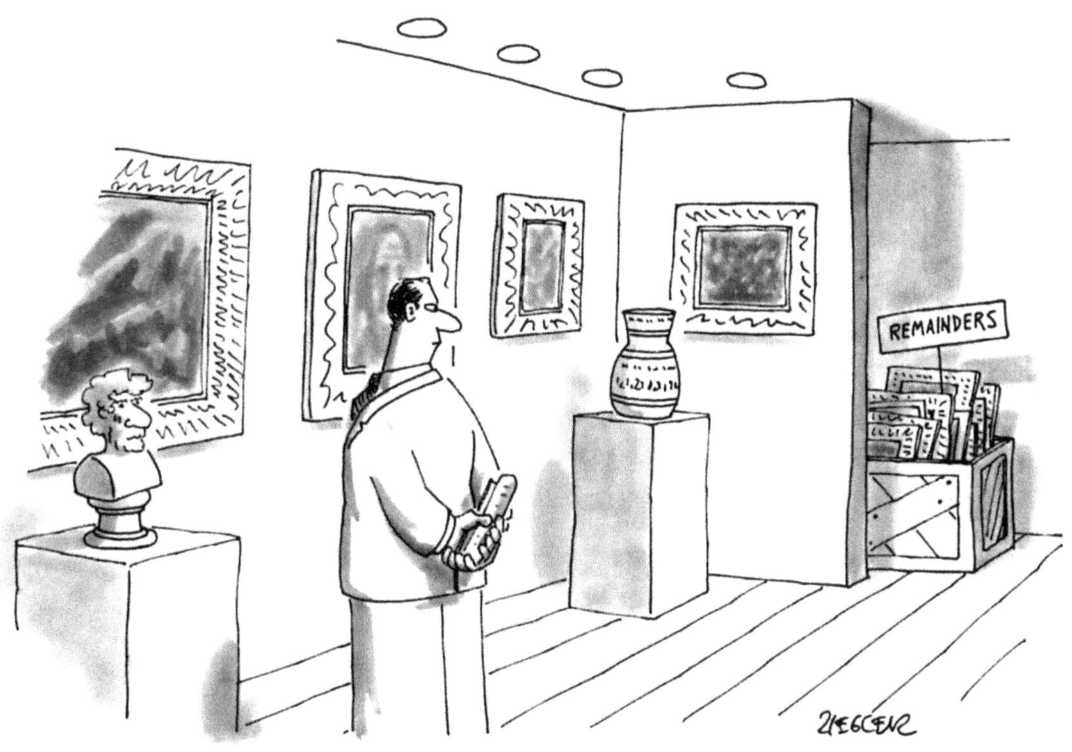
REMAINDERS

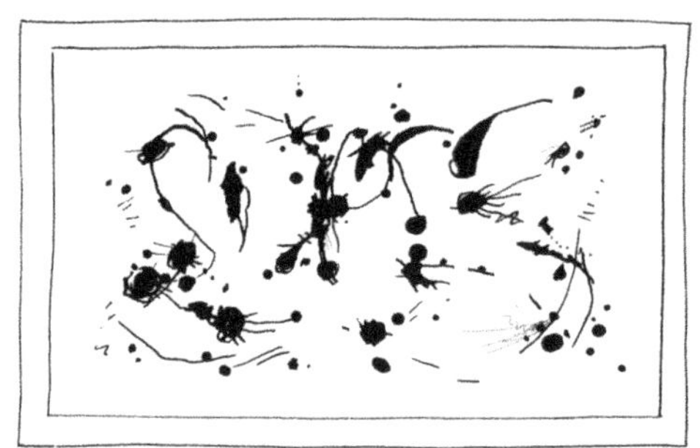

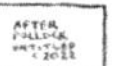
AFTER
POLLOCK

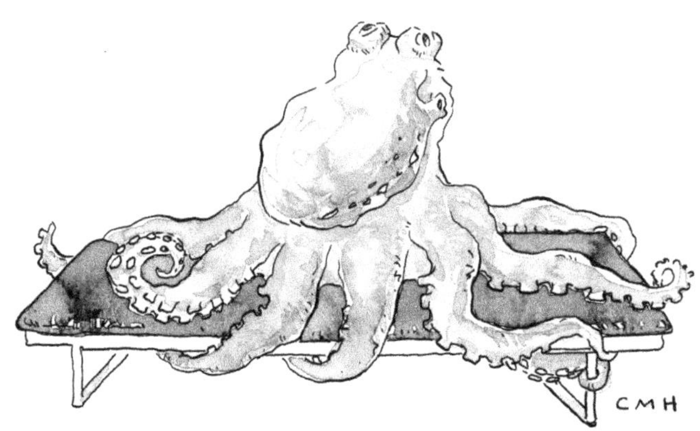
CMH

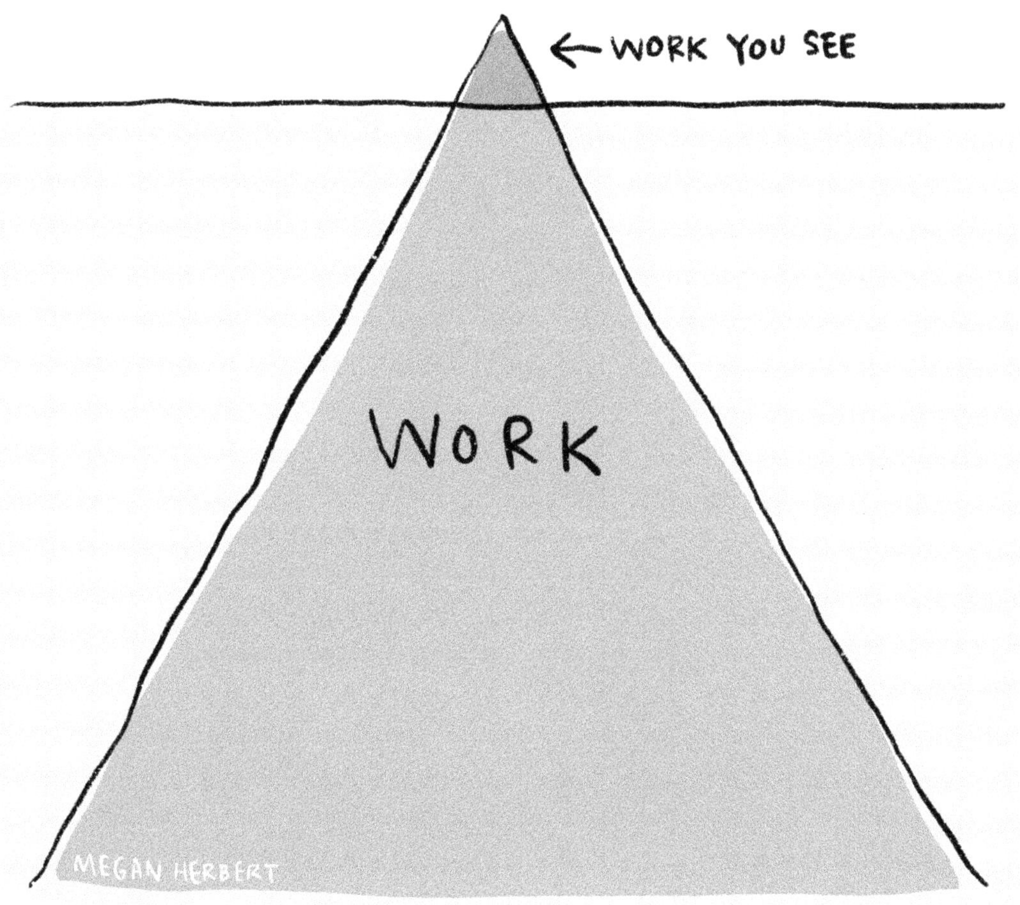

"The life of an artist."

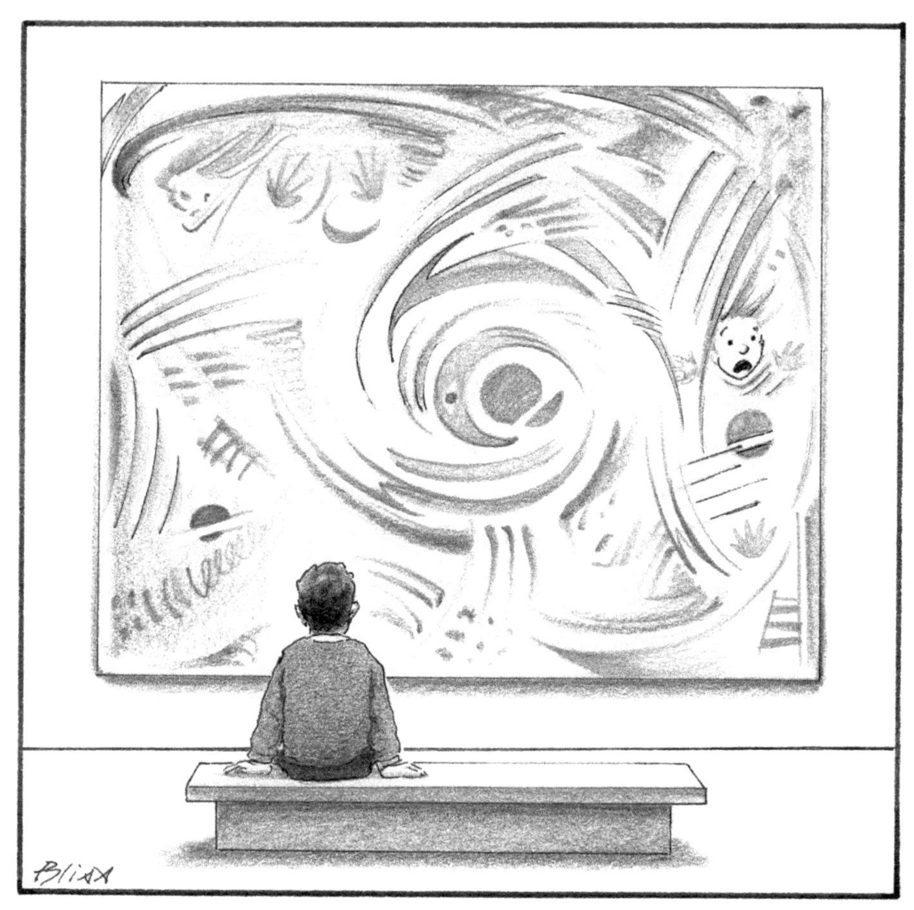

"It's almost as if you can get lost in it, Timmy. Timmy?"

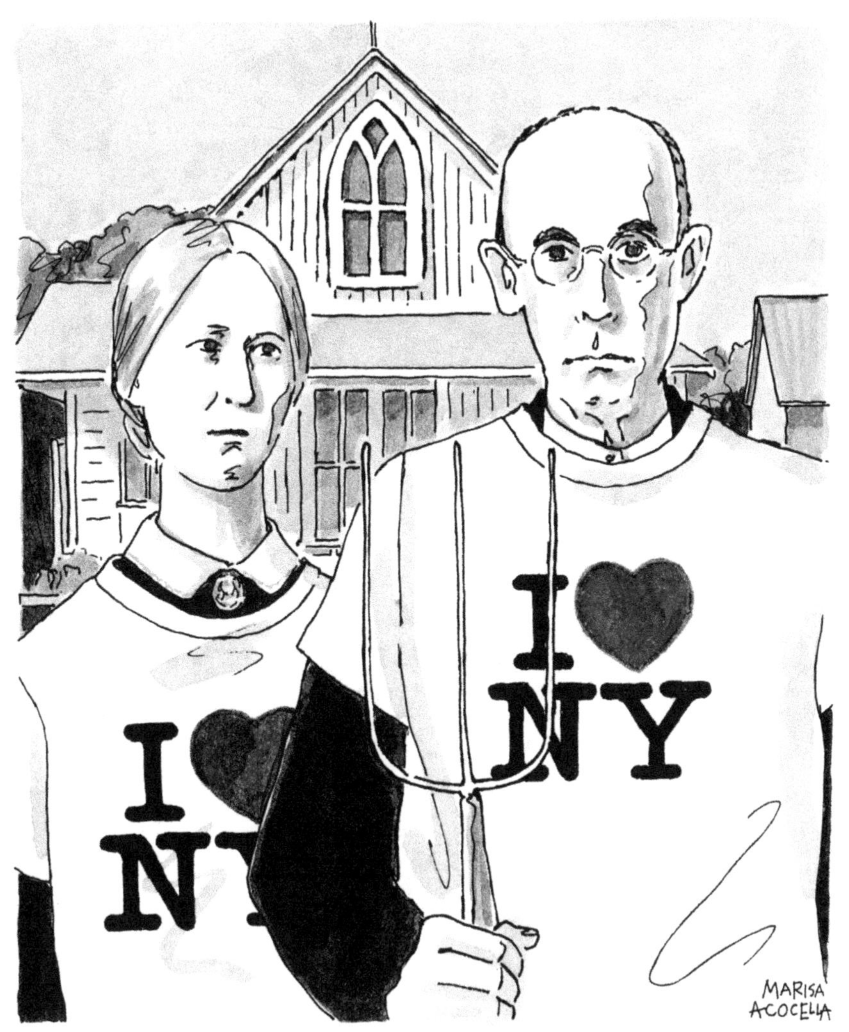
I ♥ NY
I ♥ NY
MARISA ACOCELLA

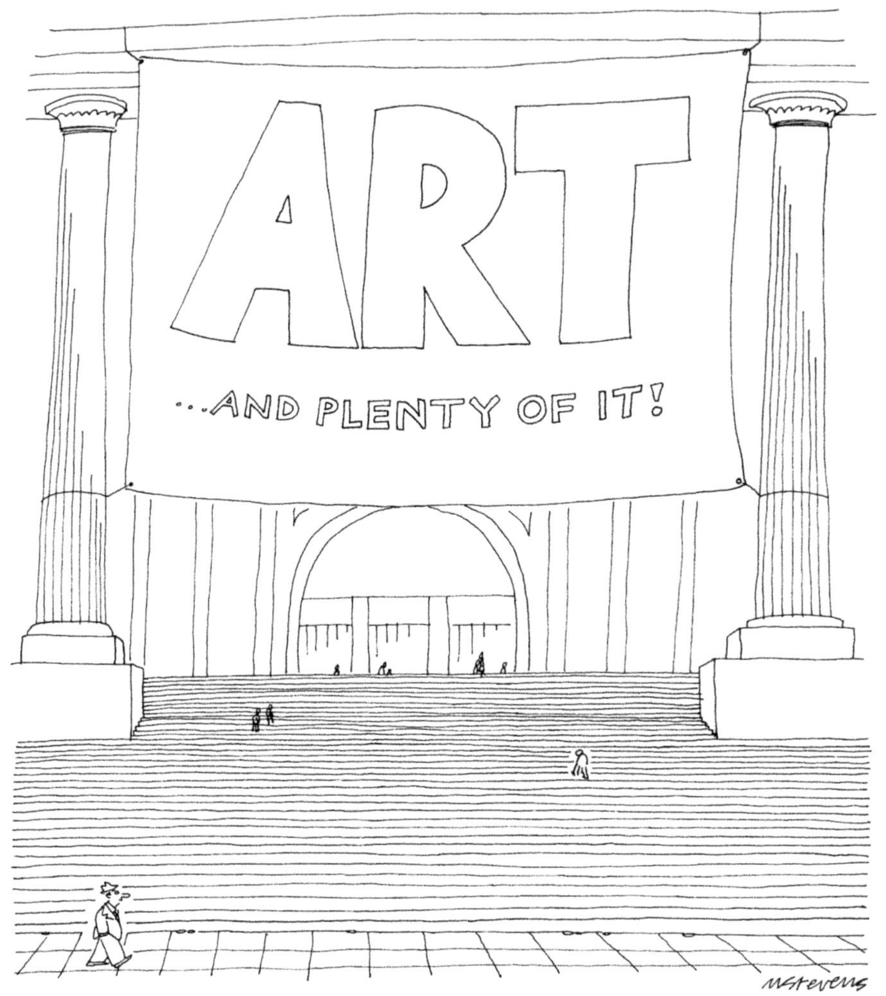
ART
...AND PLENTY OF IT!
MStevens

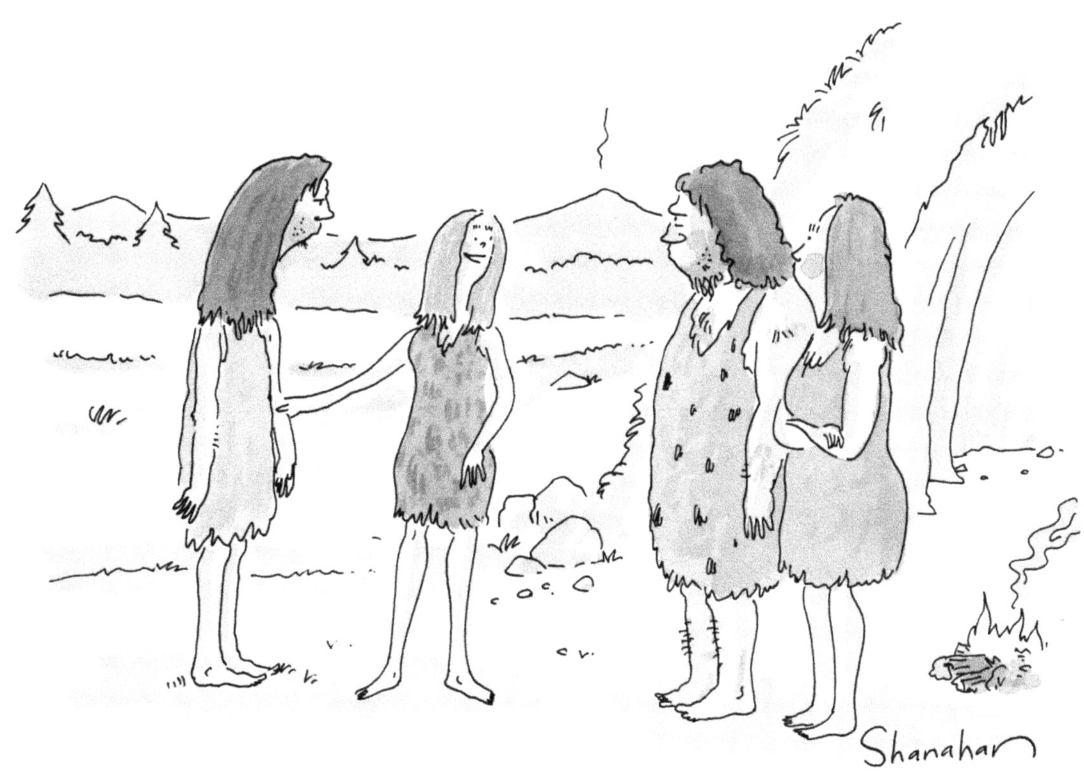

"Kip paints caves."

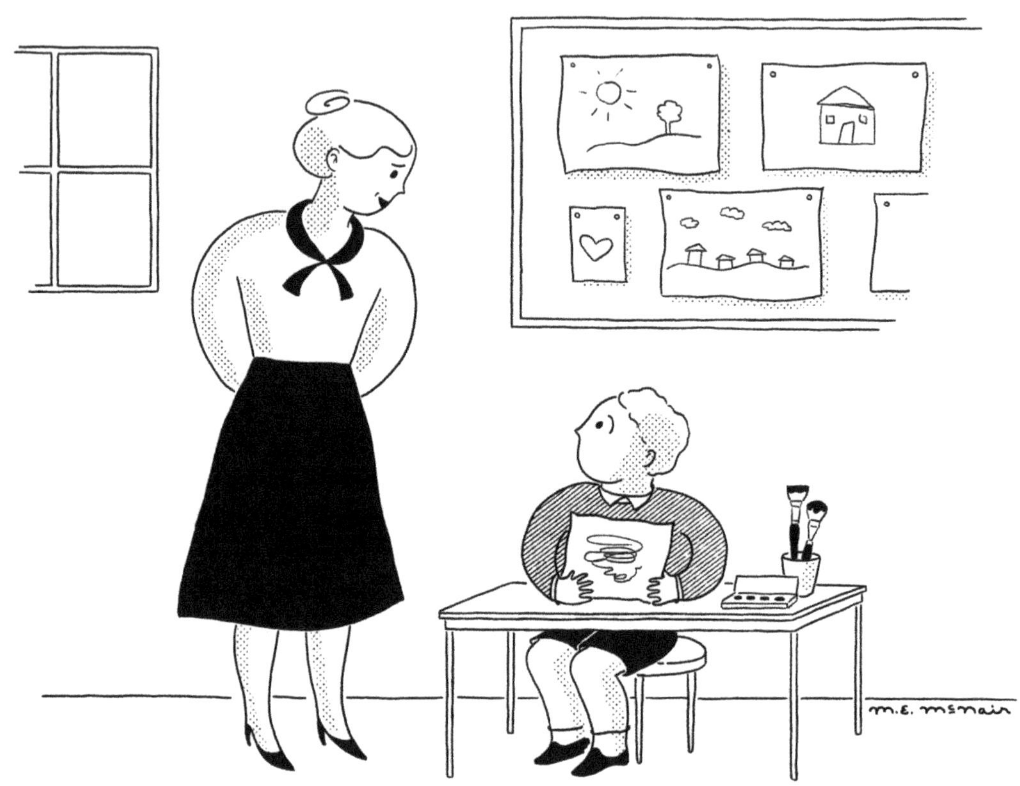

"Very creative, but is it something your mother would want to share on social media?"

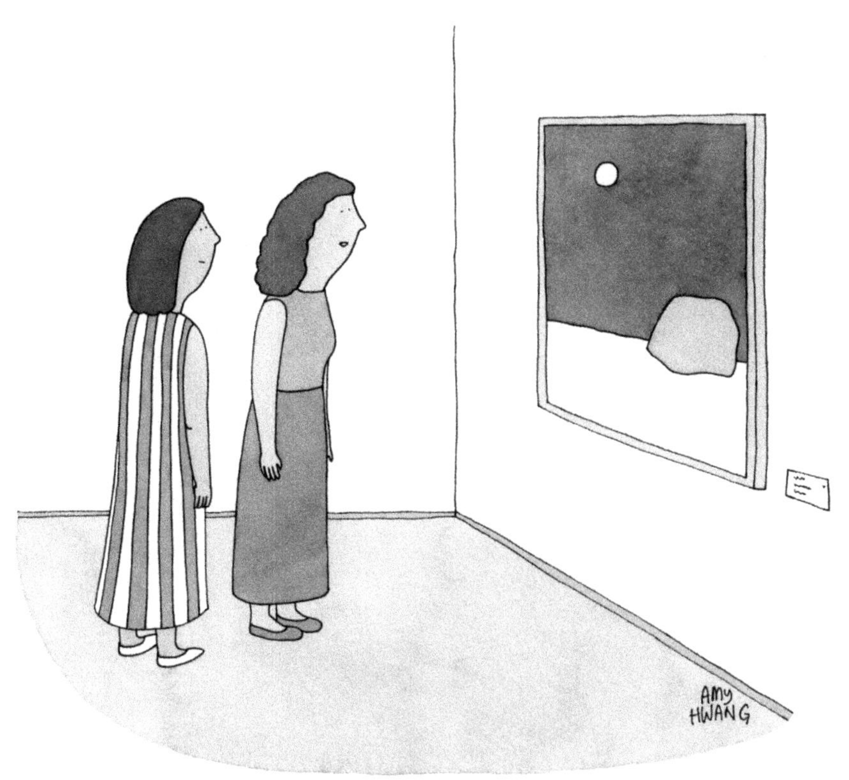

"We're lucky to live in a city with so much unaffordable art."

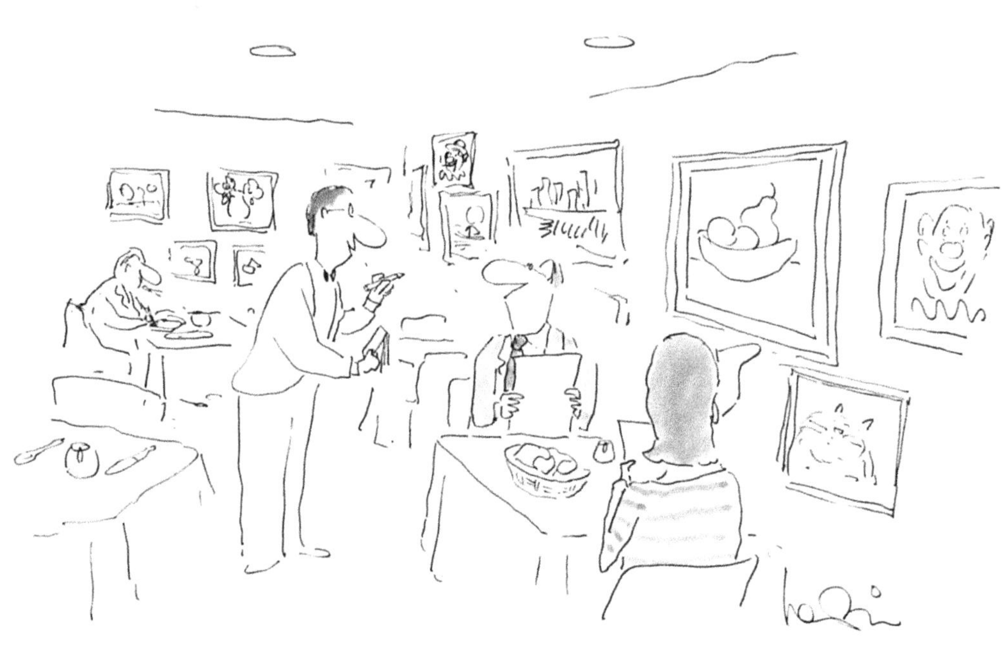

"Dinner comes complete with coffee and your choice of dessert or an oil painting."

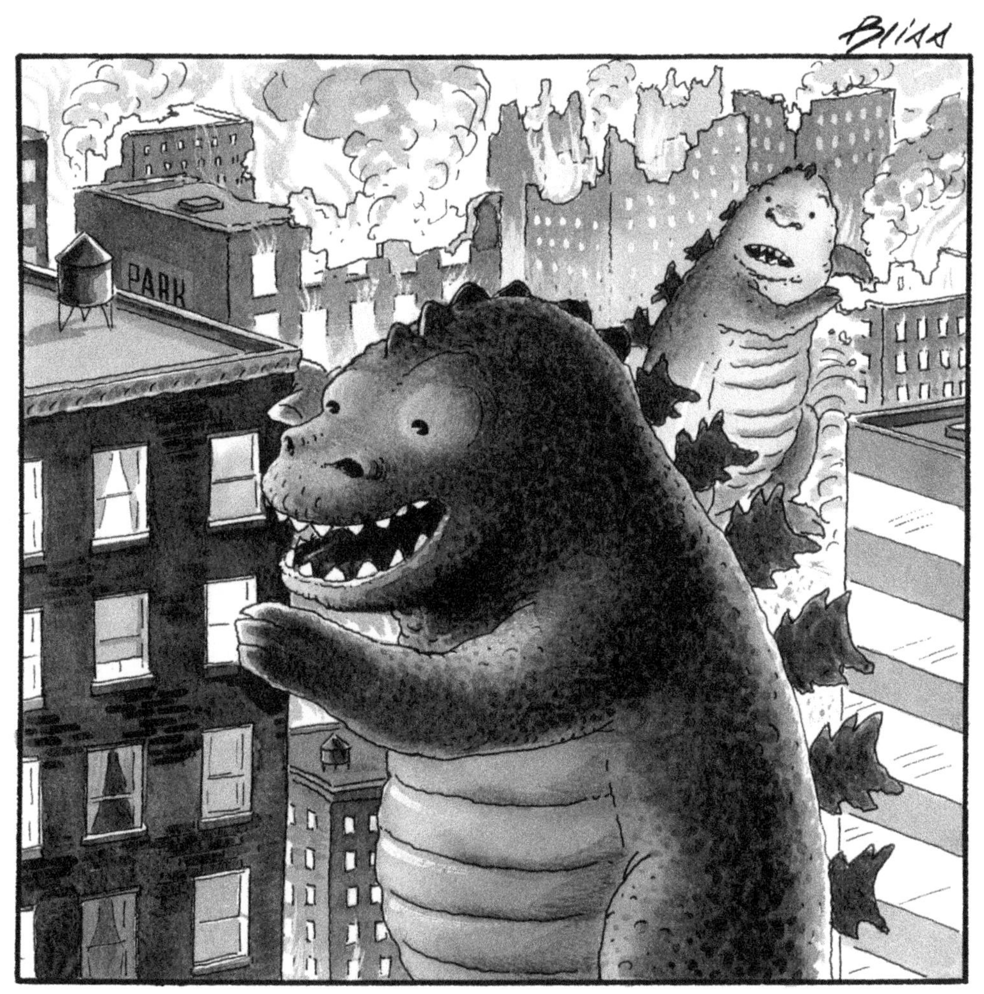

"Lou, c'm'ere—you gotta check out this guy's Degas!"

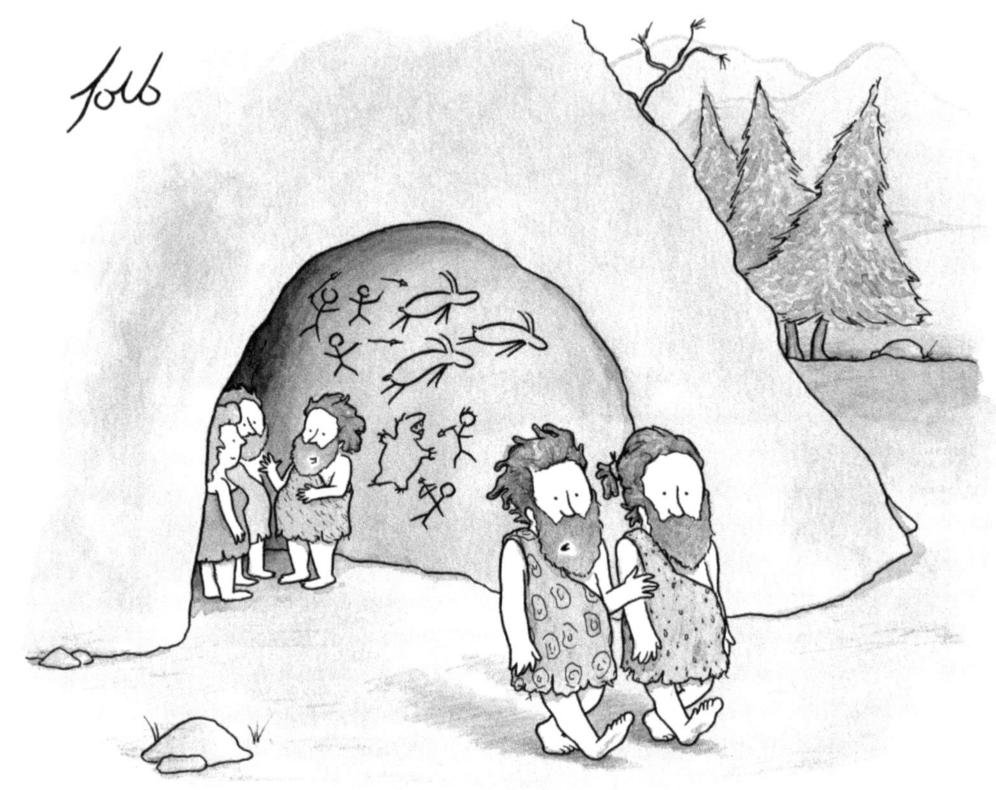

"He's done it all. There's nothing left to draw."

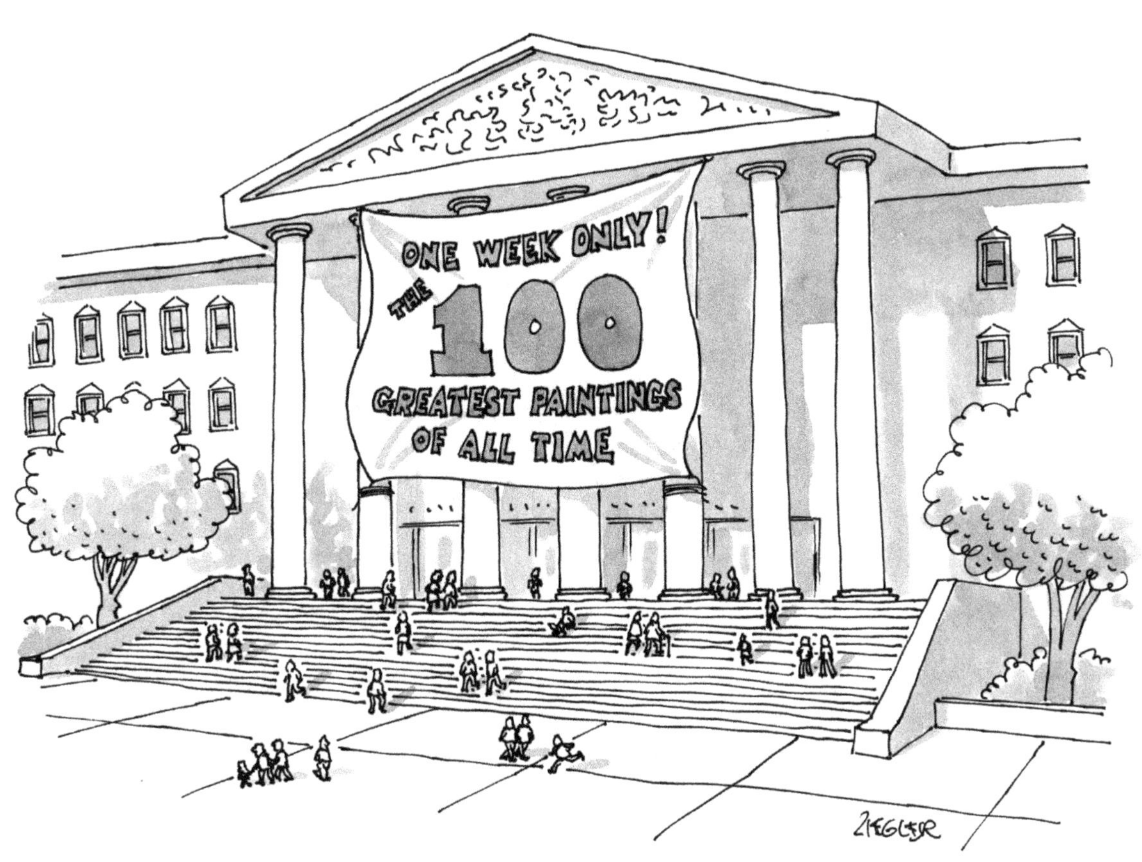
ONE WEEK ONLY!
THE 100
GREATEST PAINTINGS
OF ALL TIME
ZIEGLER

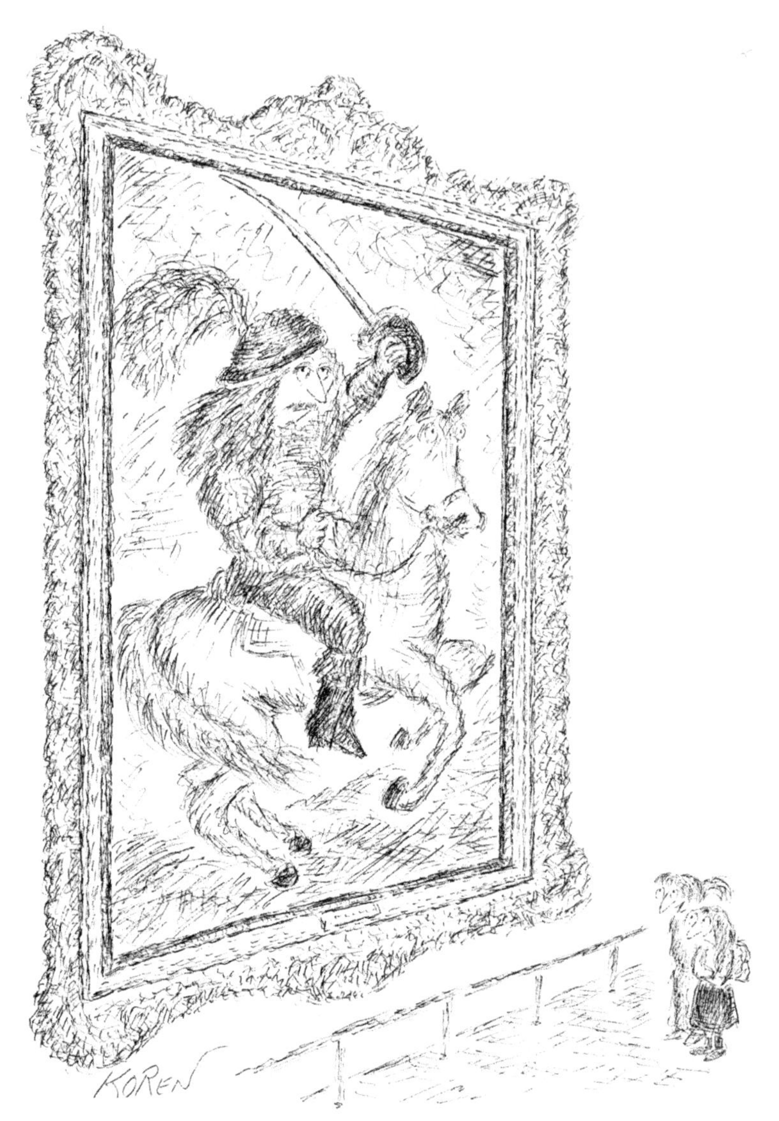

"I think he was a celebrity."

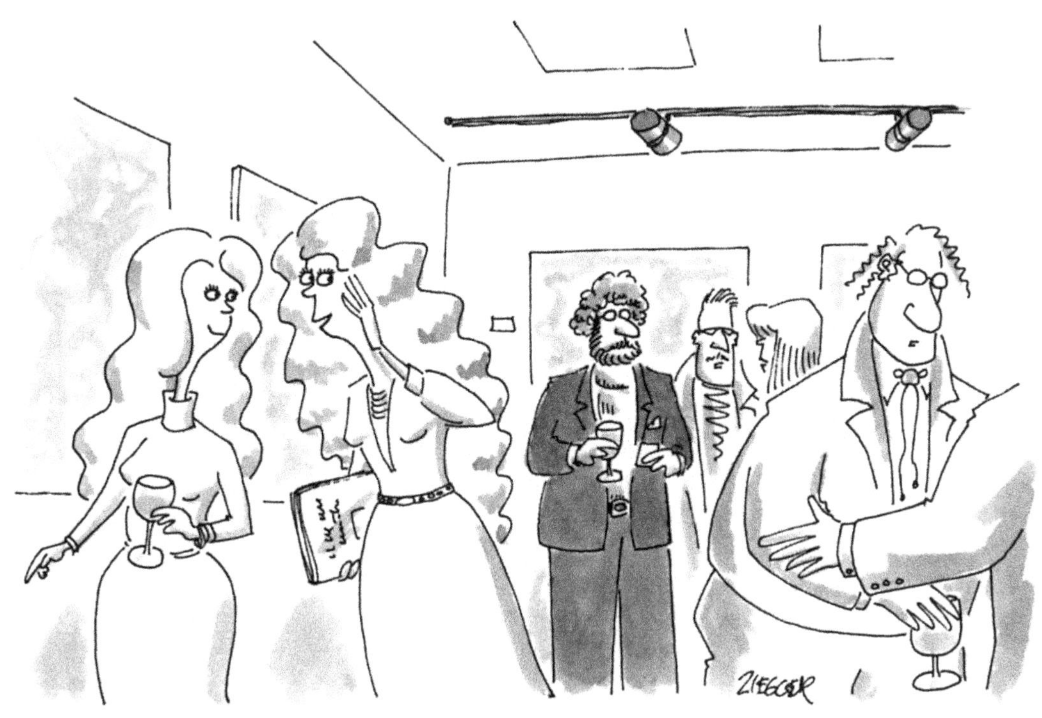

"Artsy. But not fartsy."

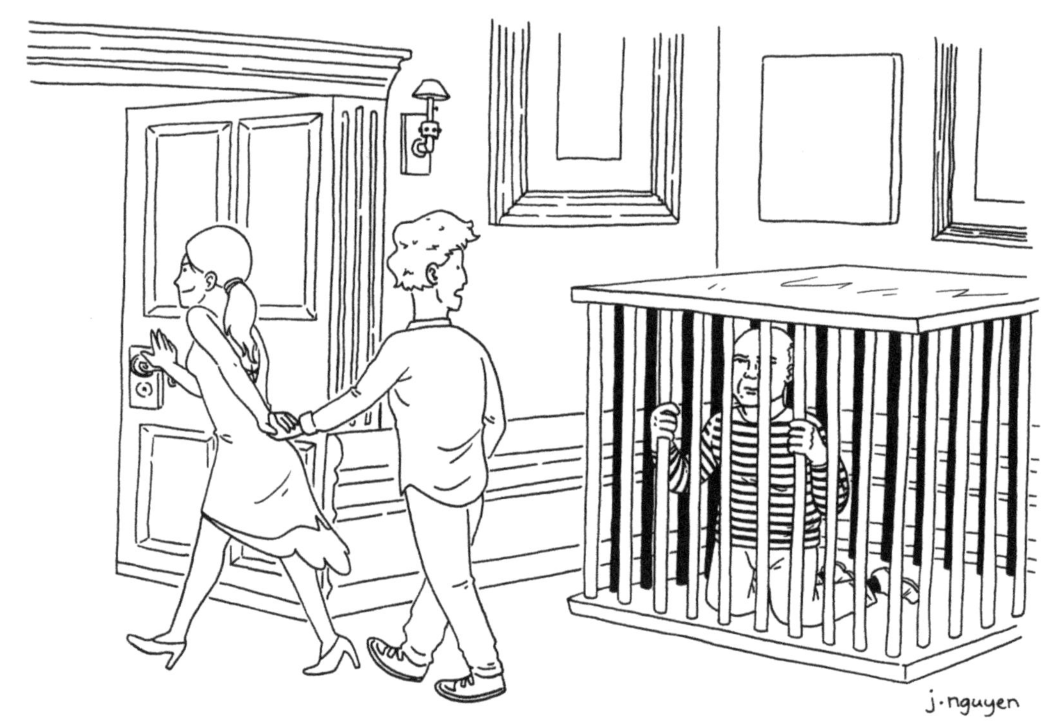

"You have a Picasso?"

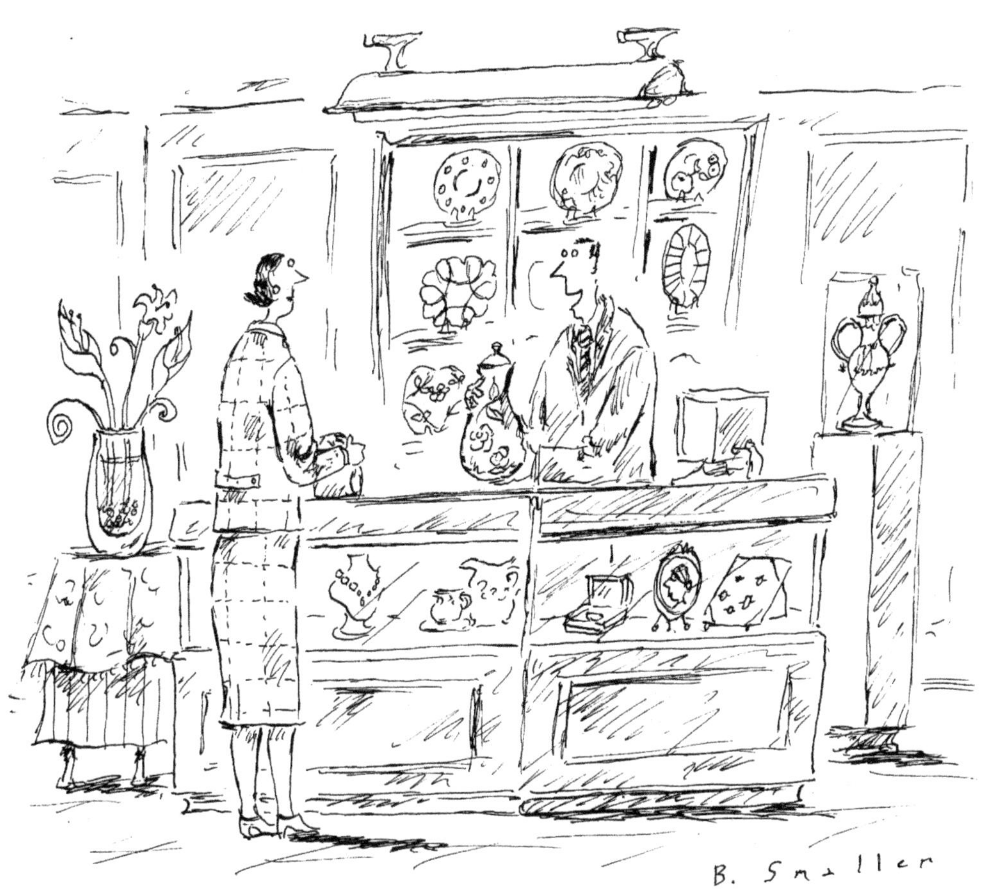

"It's museum-store quality."

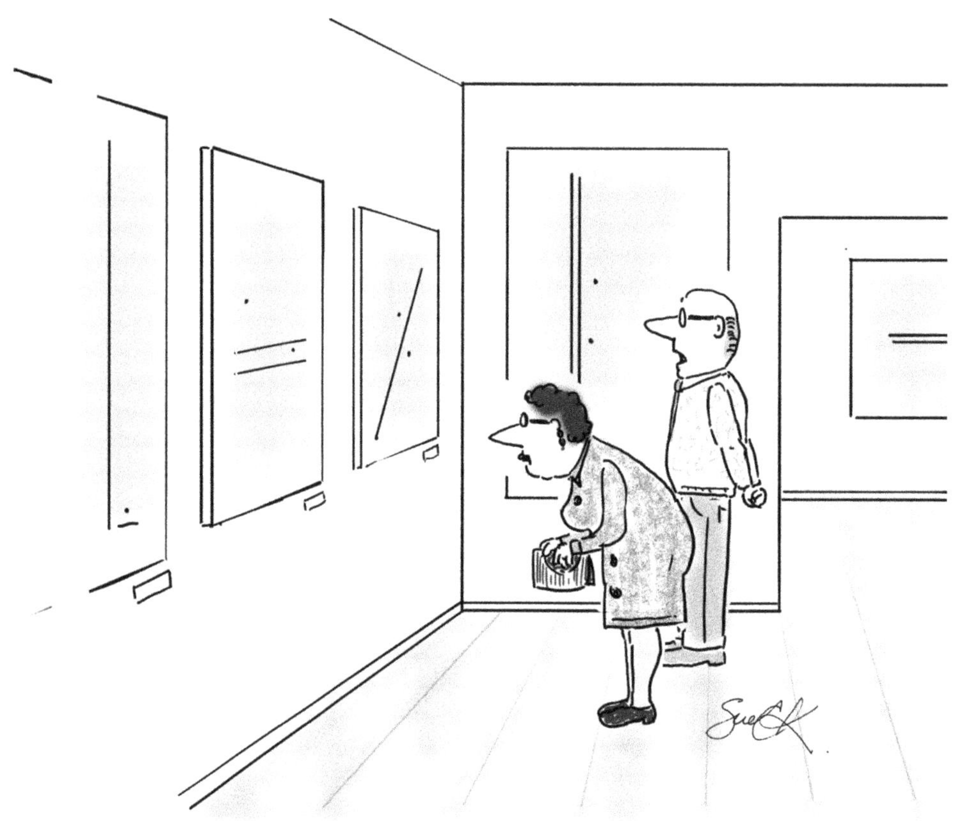

"By 'genius' do they mean the artist or the marketing department?"

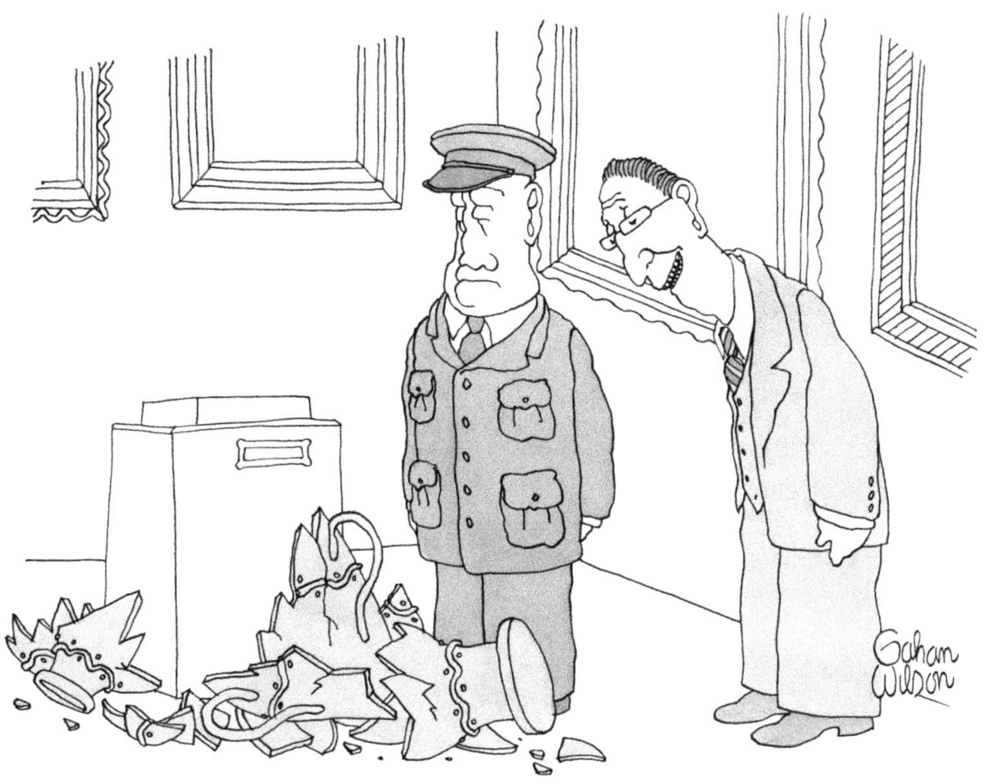

"Fortunately, I think we have an extremely accurate copy of it in the museum's gift shop."

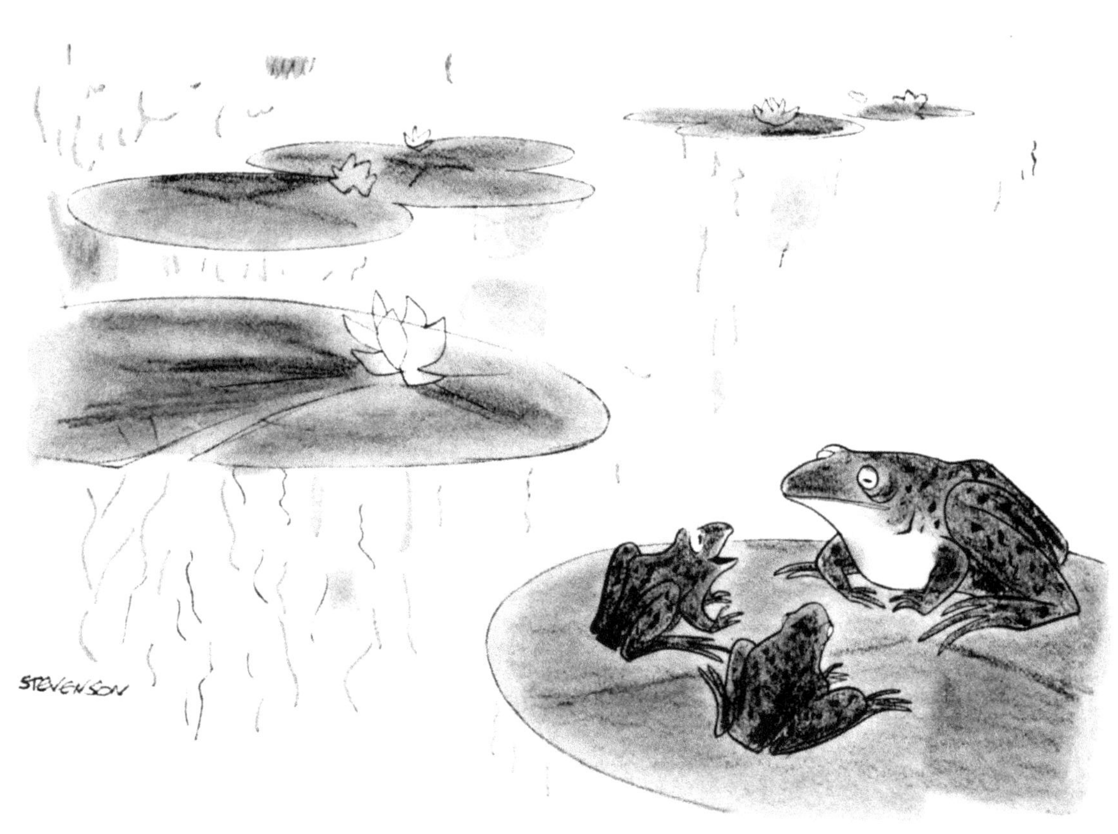

"Tell us again about Monet, Grandpa."

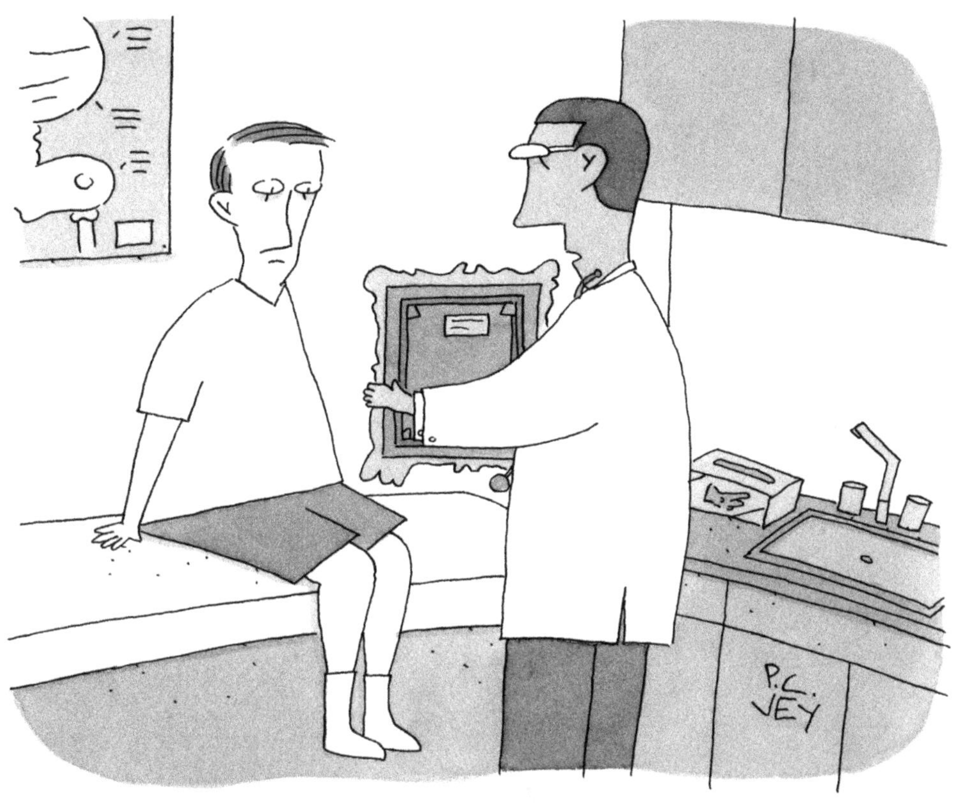

"Studies show that people who allow art into their lives can substantially reduce their dependency on selective seretonin reuptake inhibitors."

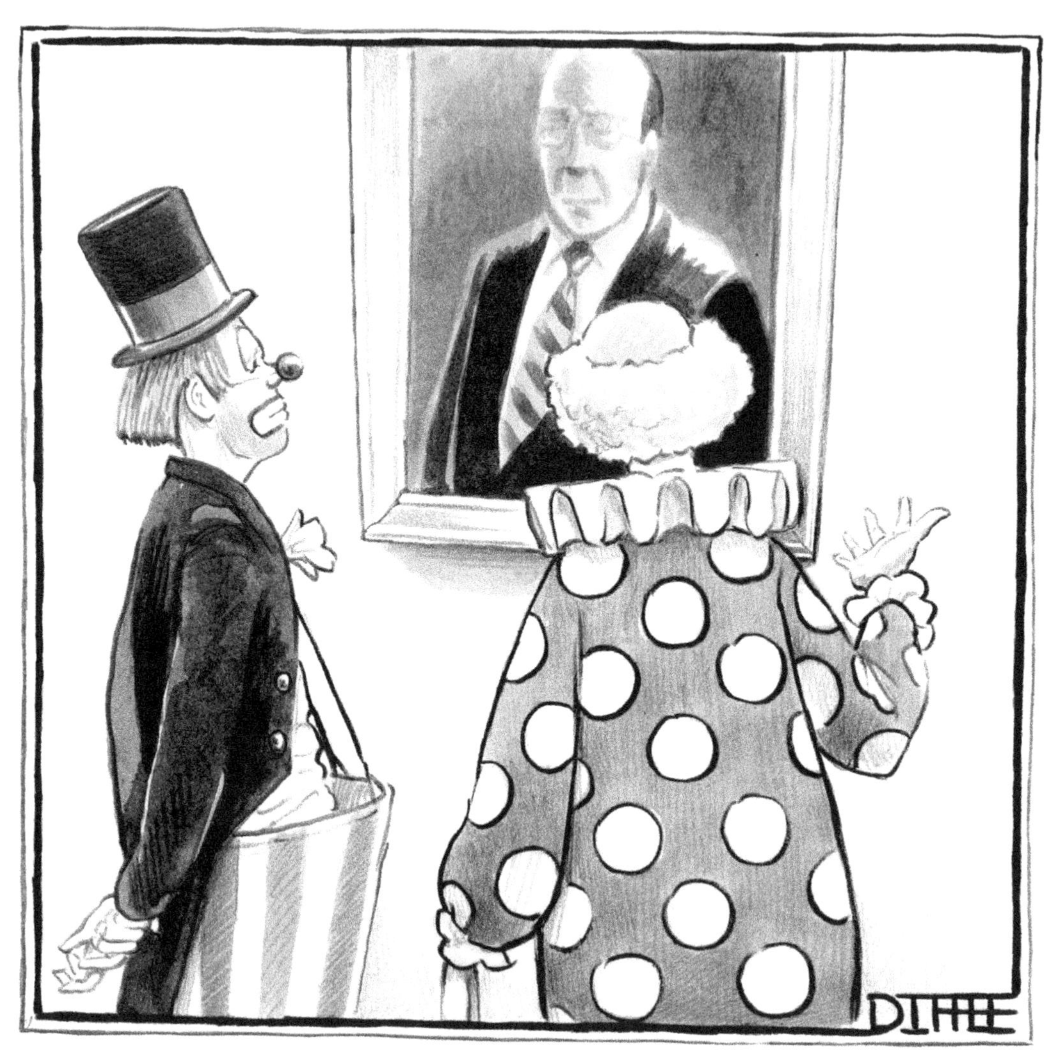

"I always find paintings like this a little bit creepy."

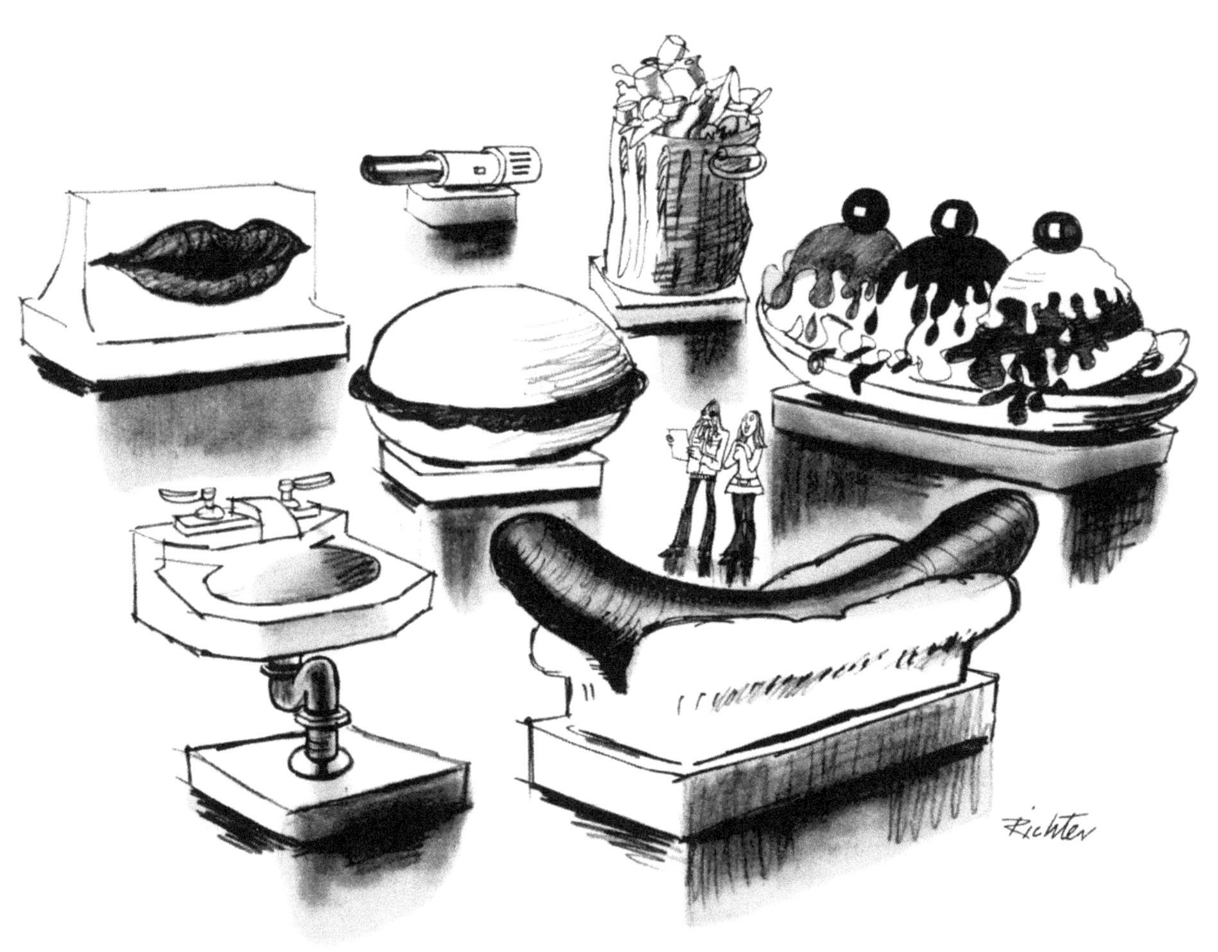

"Wow! You mean they got all of this in exchange for just one van Gogh?"

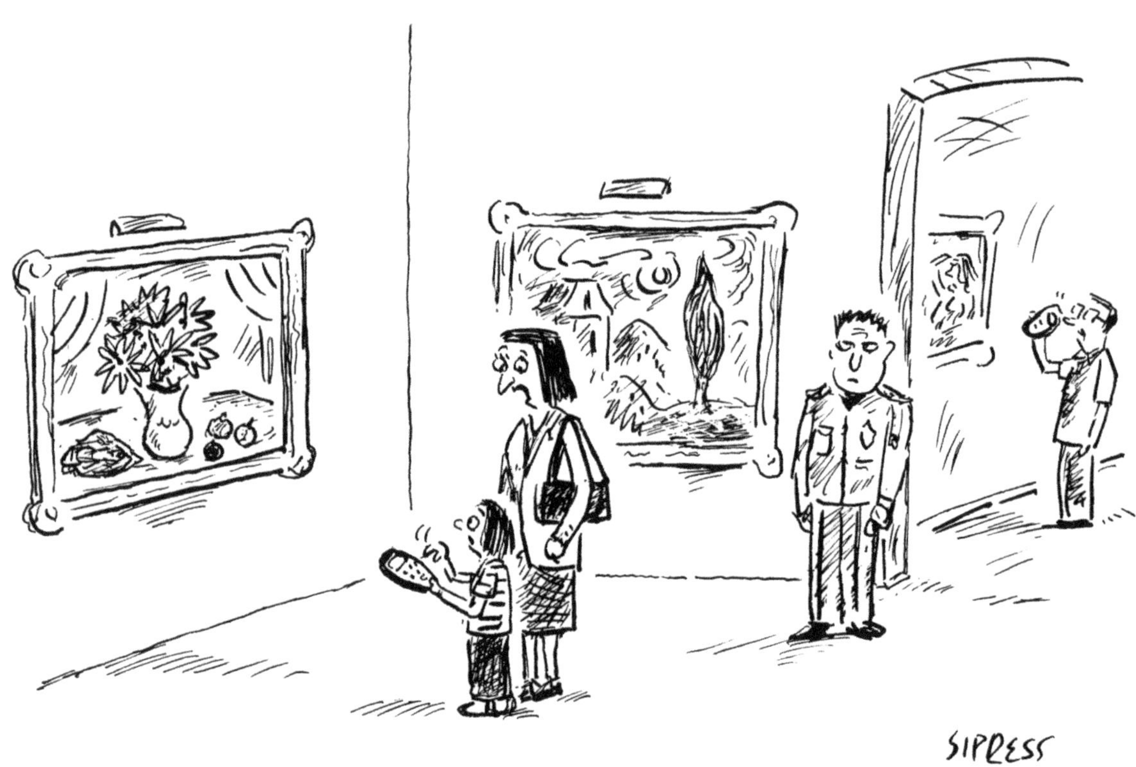

"It's an audio guide, sweetheart, not a remote."

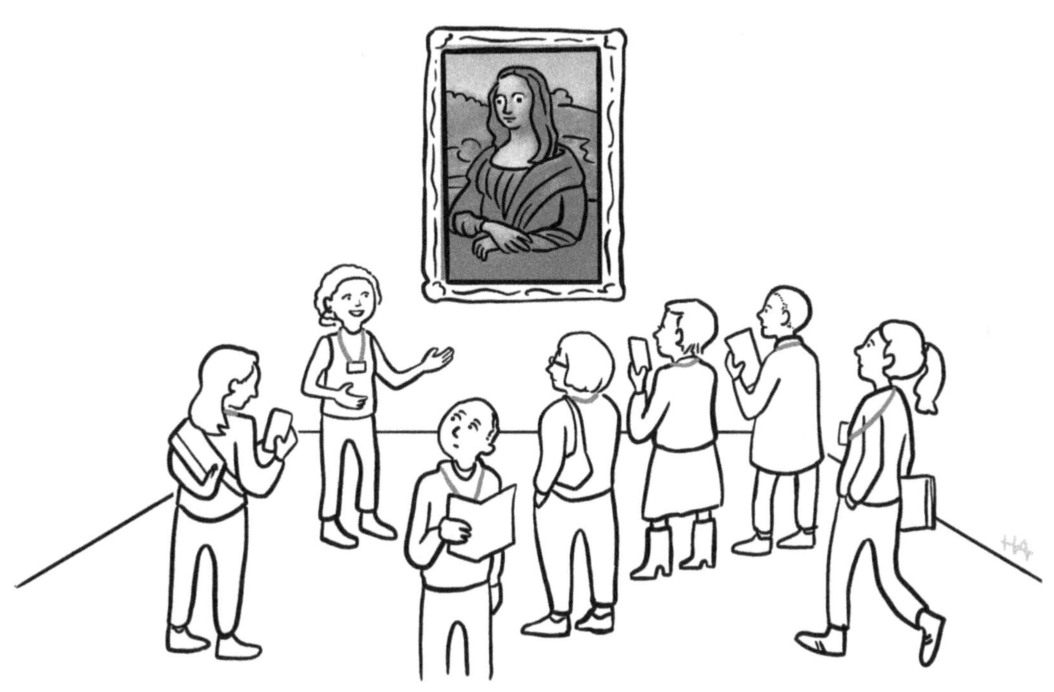

"Notice how her eyes follow your bluetooth-enabled visitor badges around the room?"

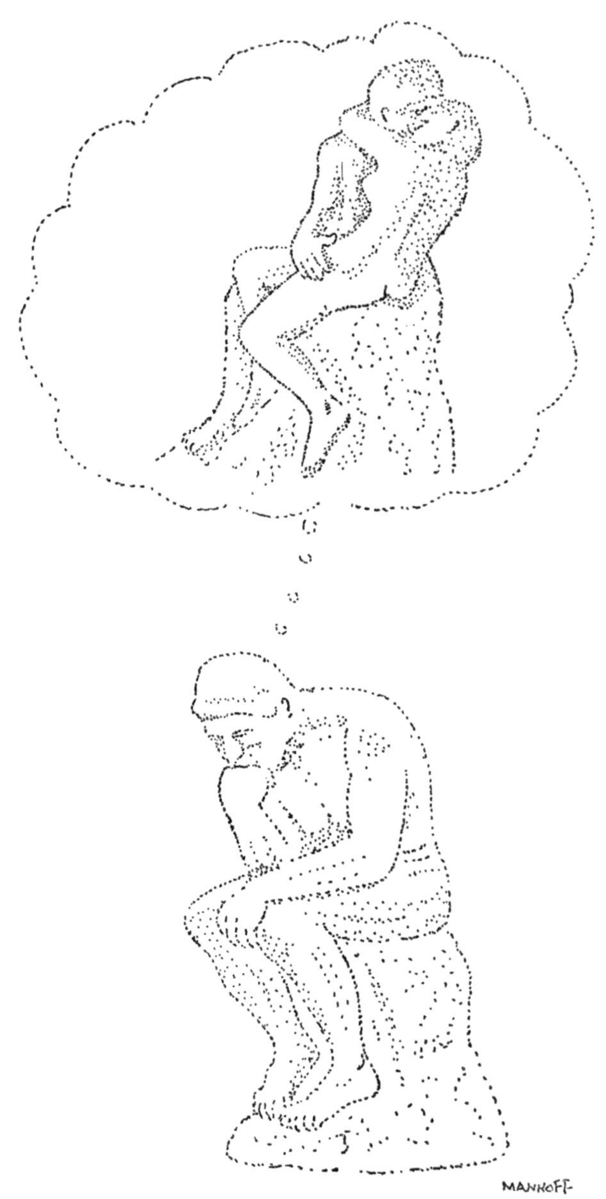
MANKOFF

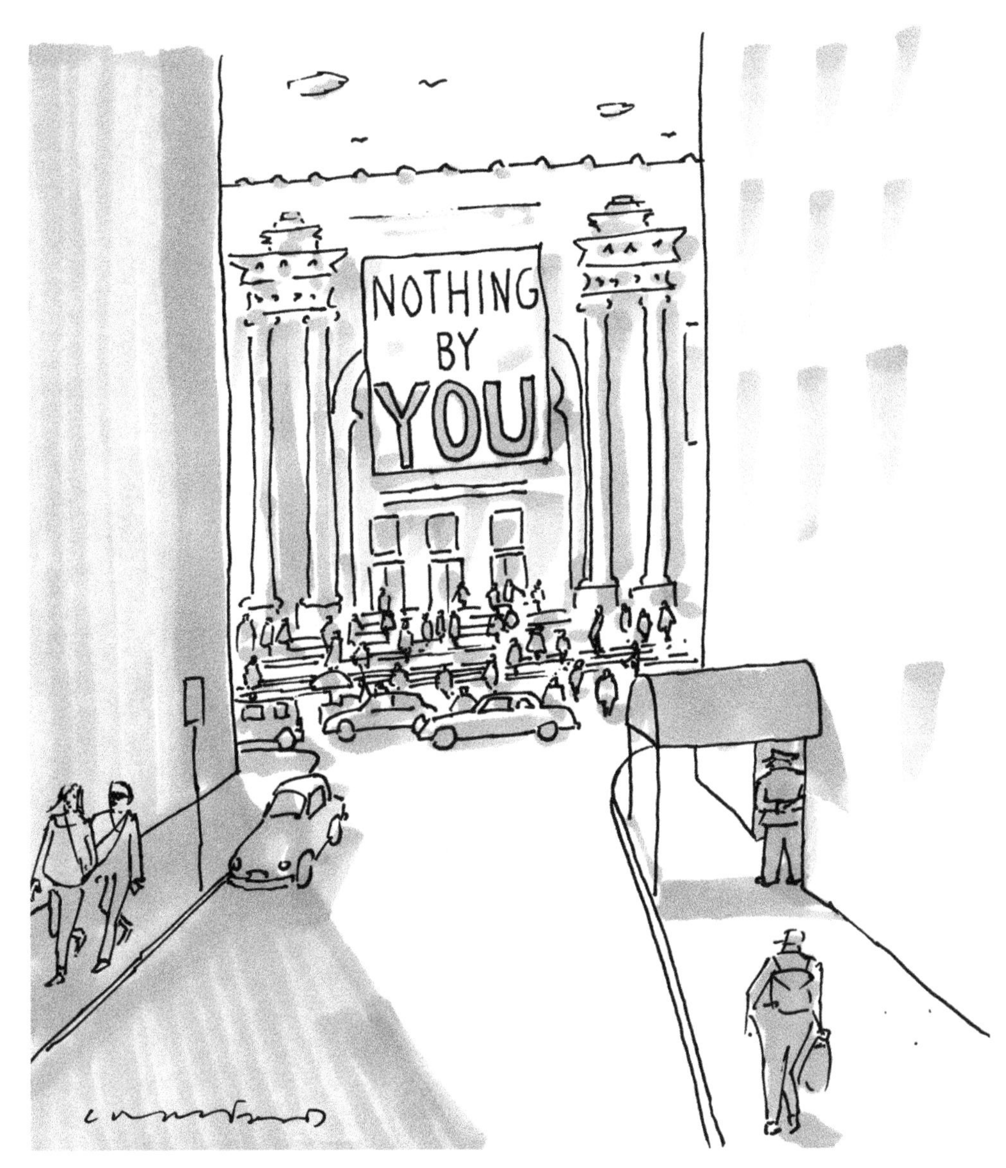
NOTHING
BY
YOU

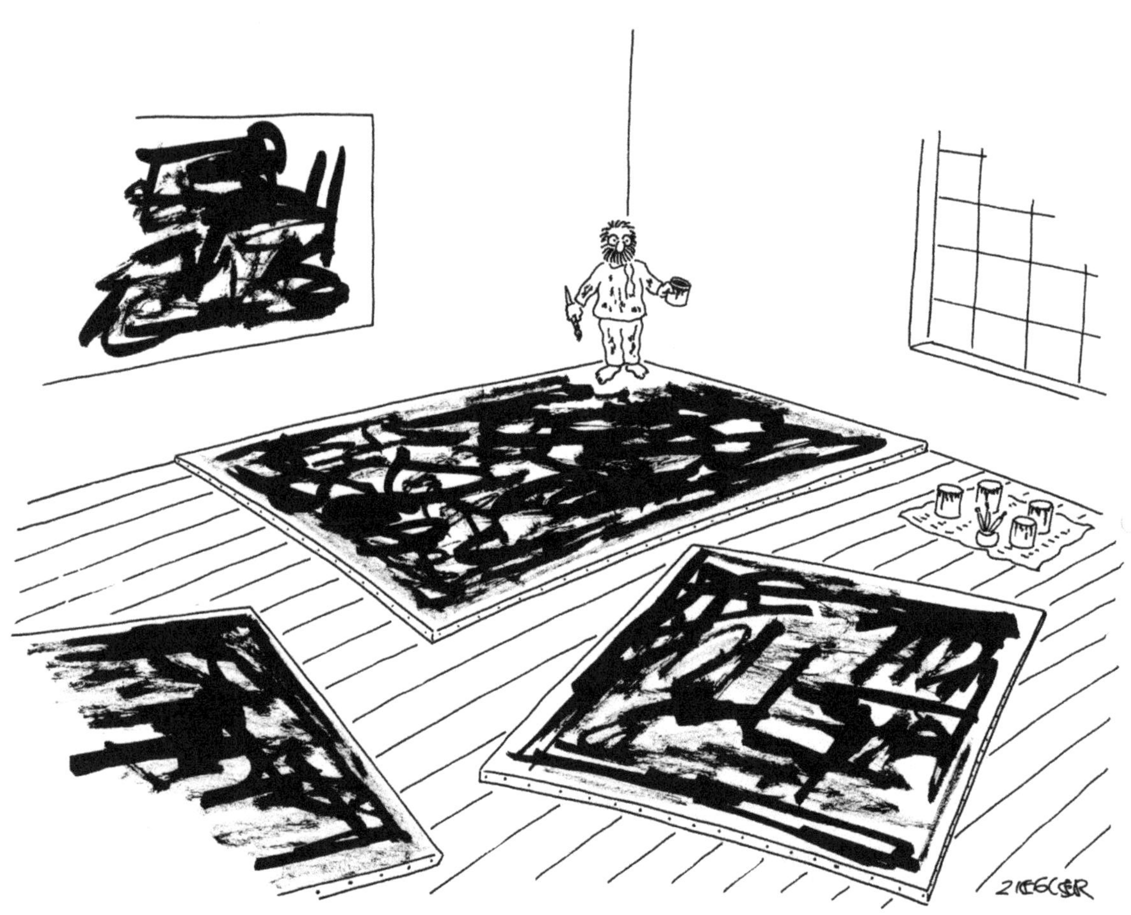

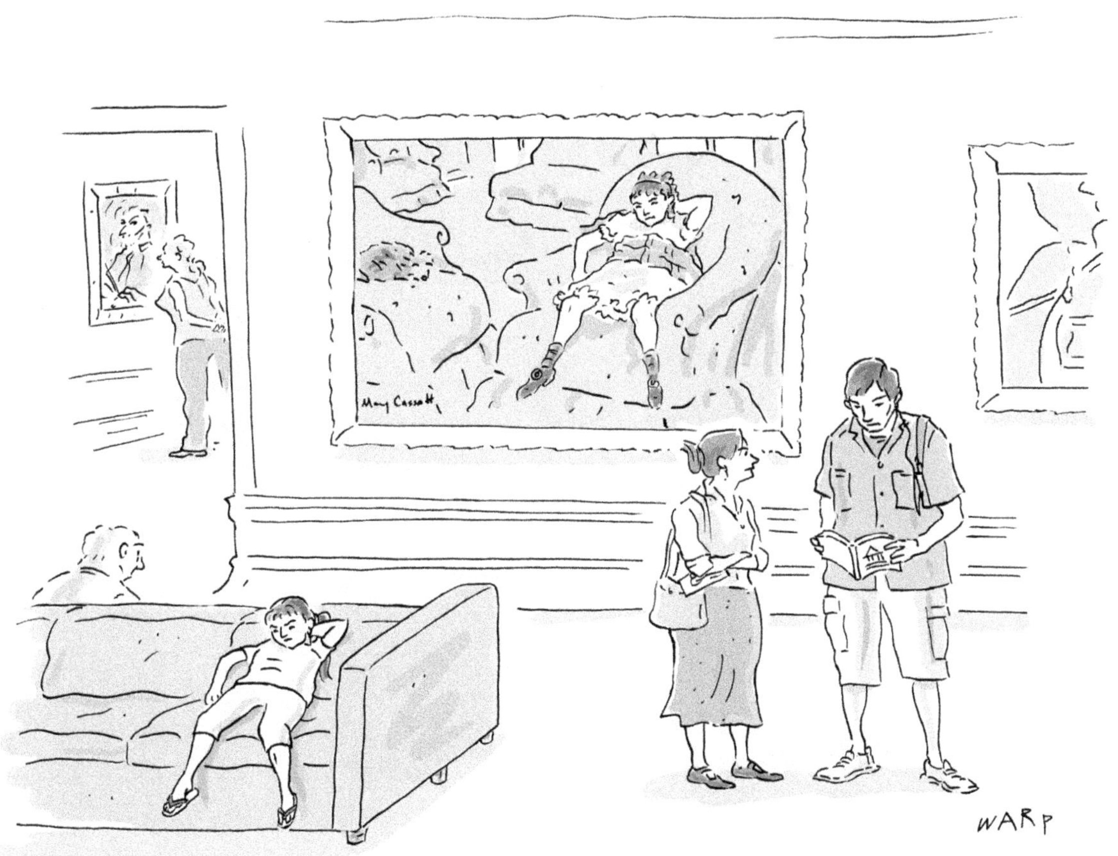
Mary Cassatt
WARP

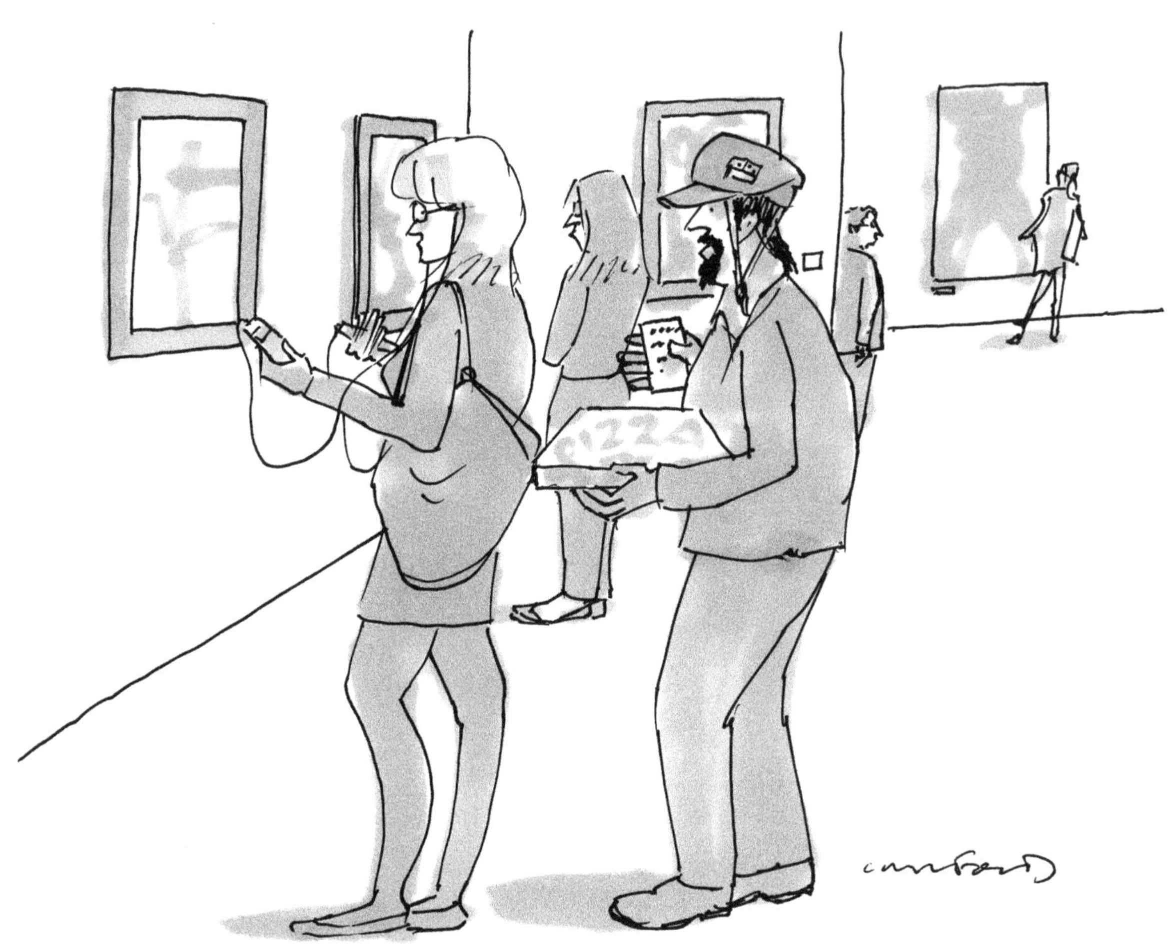

"Miss, did you order the small fiery Hawaiian with Fauve influences?"

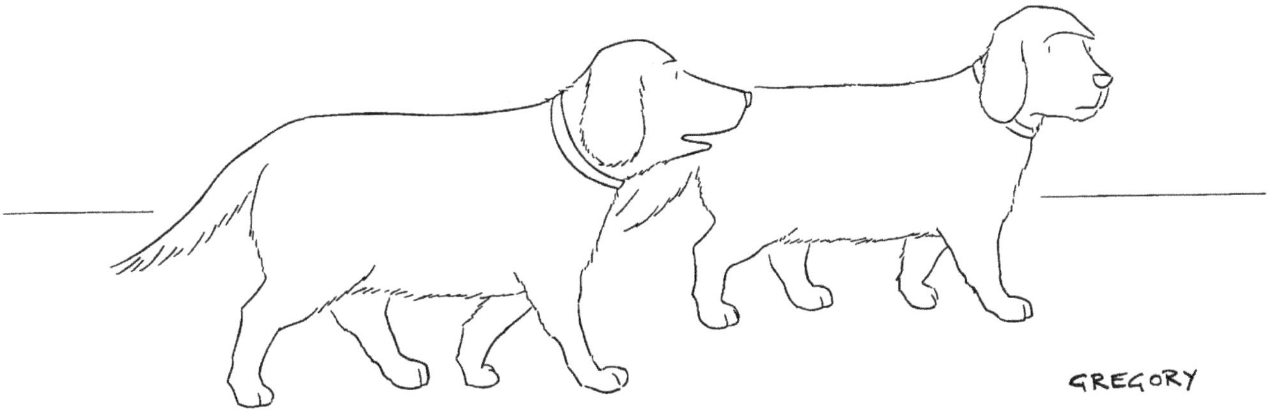

"What I do as an artist is take an ordinary object—say, a lamppost—and, by urinating on it, transform it into something that is uniquely my own."

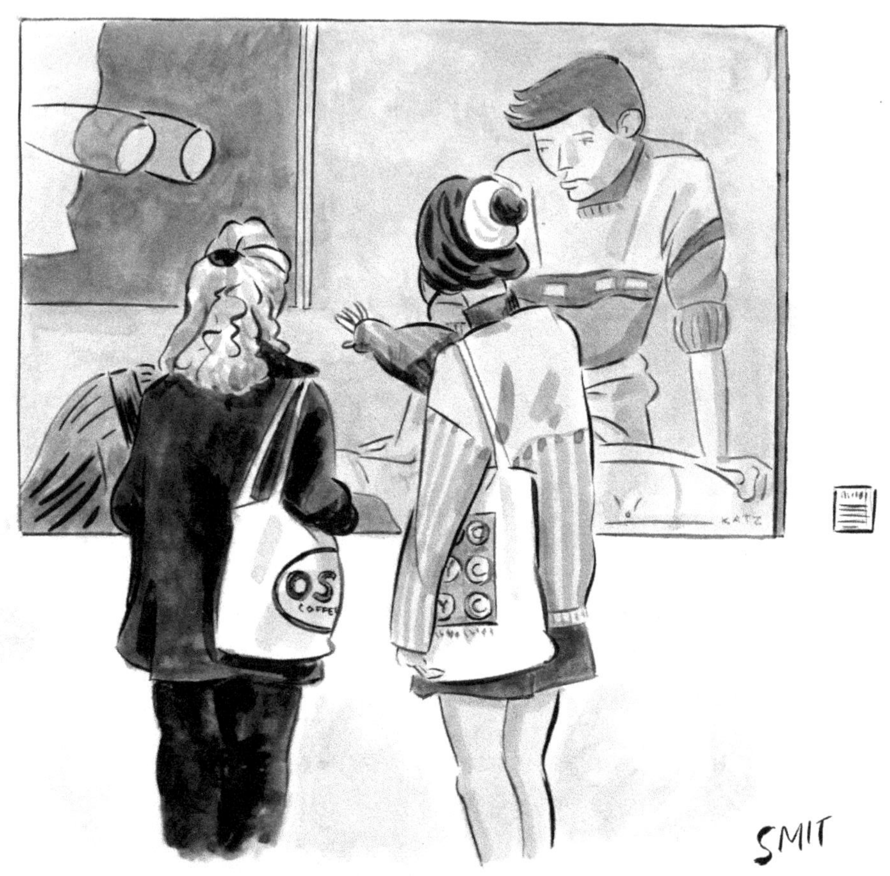

"I just think it would be a better painting if there were a short, humorous caption underneath."

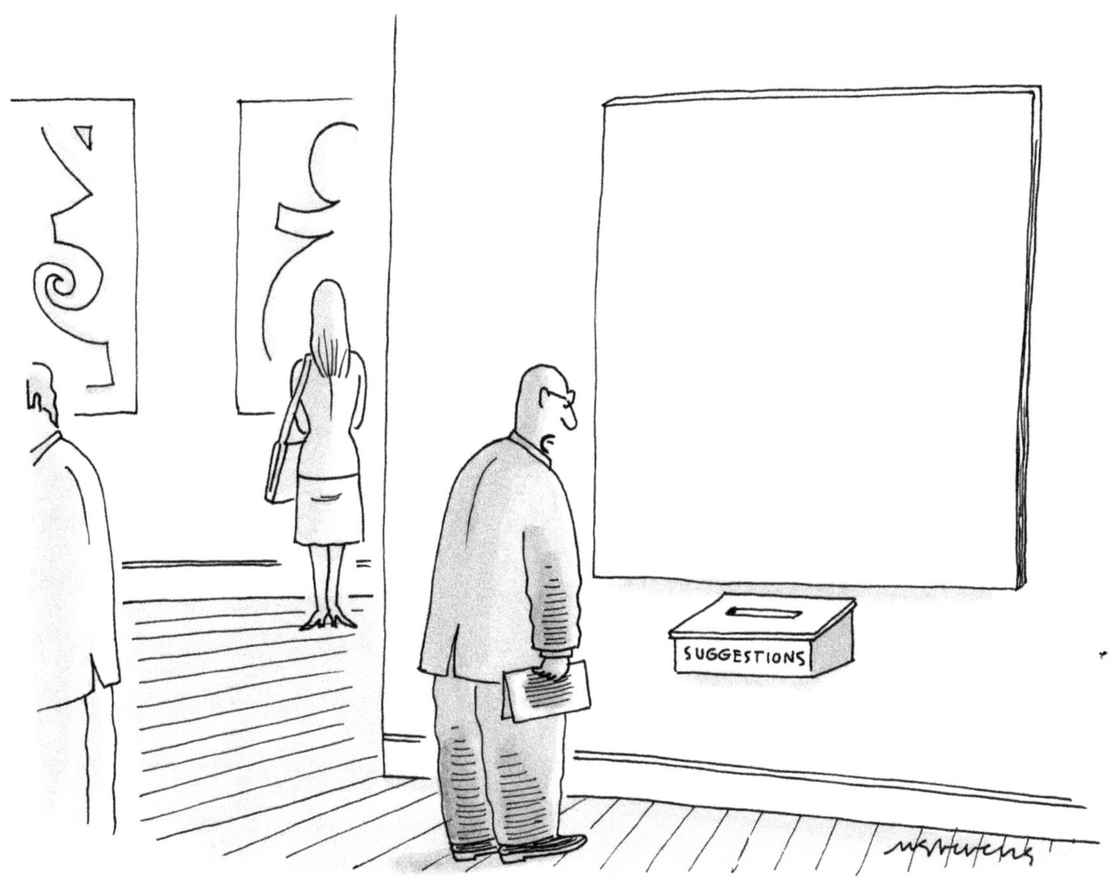
SUGGESTIONS

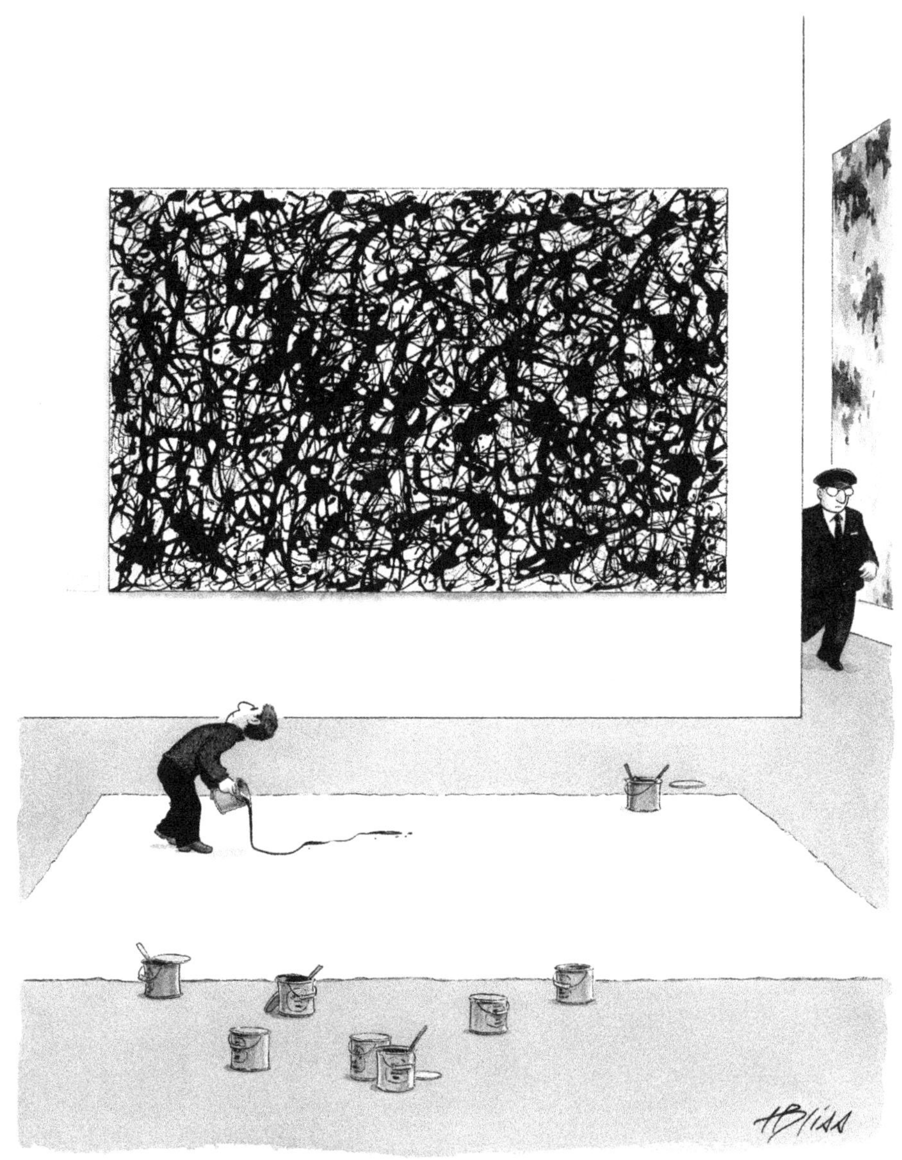

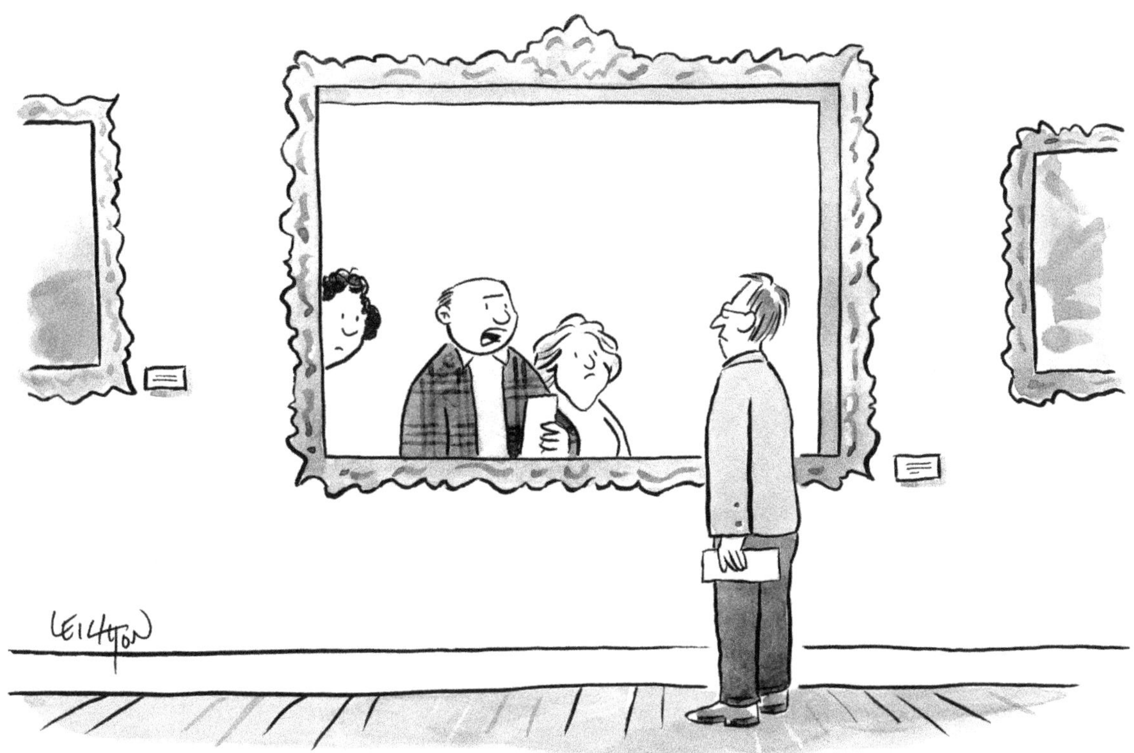

"Well, you're no masterpiece yourself."

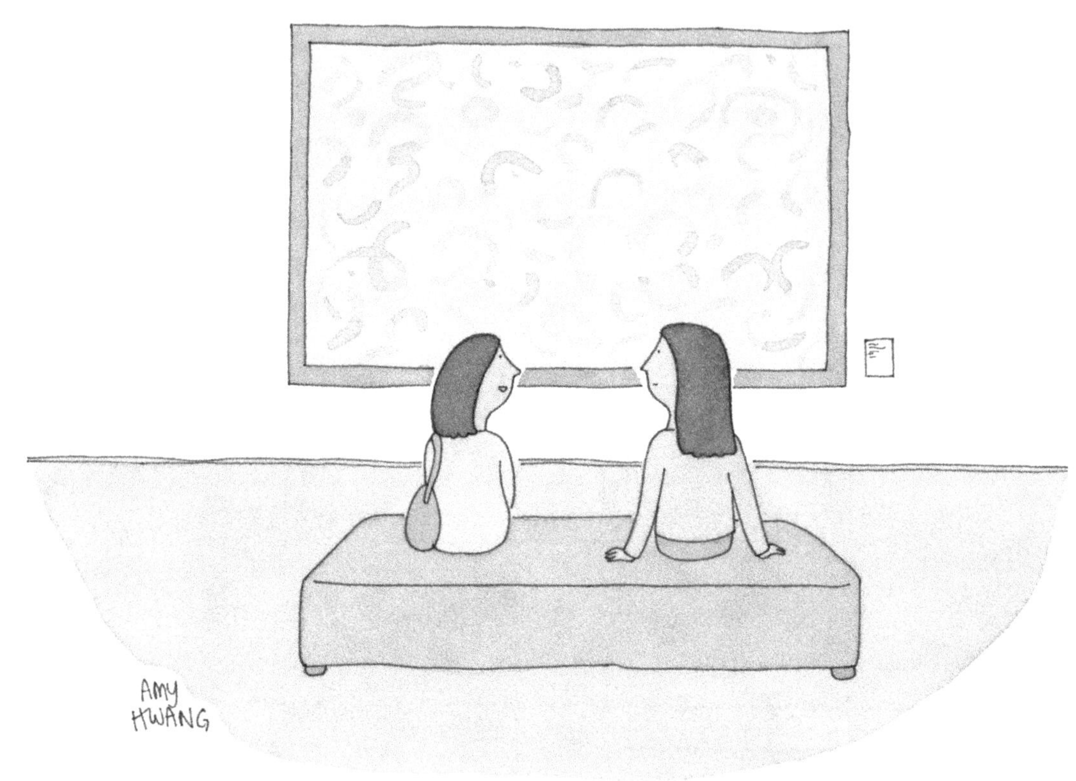

"I like this painting because it has a bench."

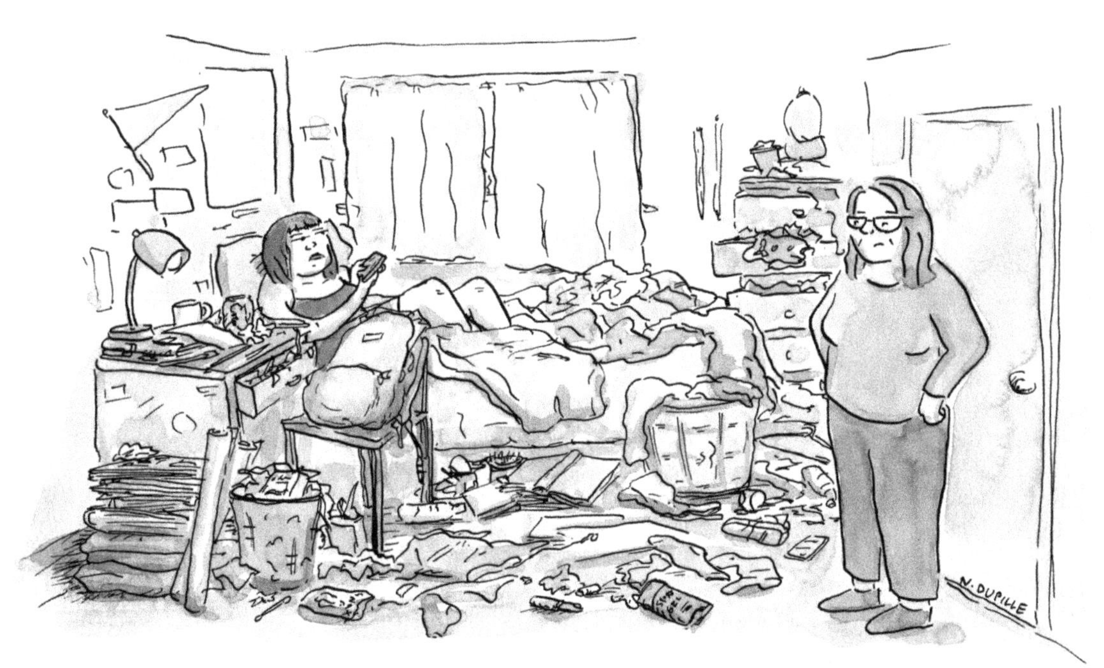

"It's actually a maximalist art installation."

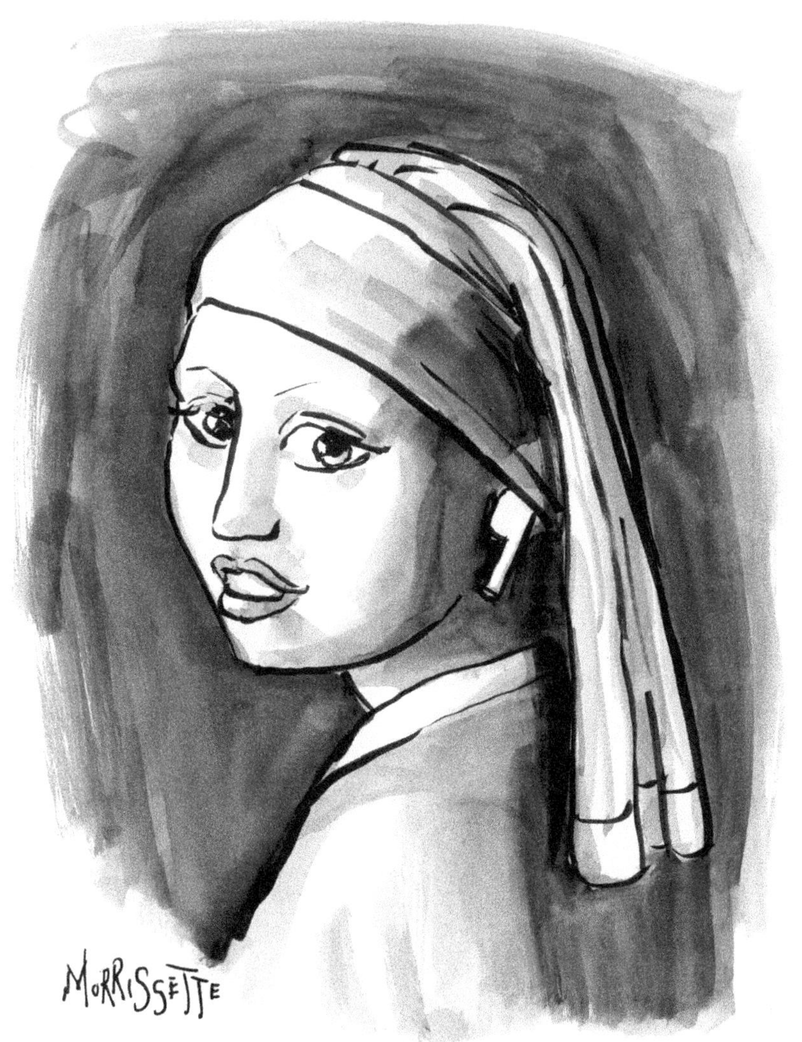
MORRISSETTE

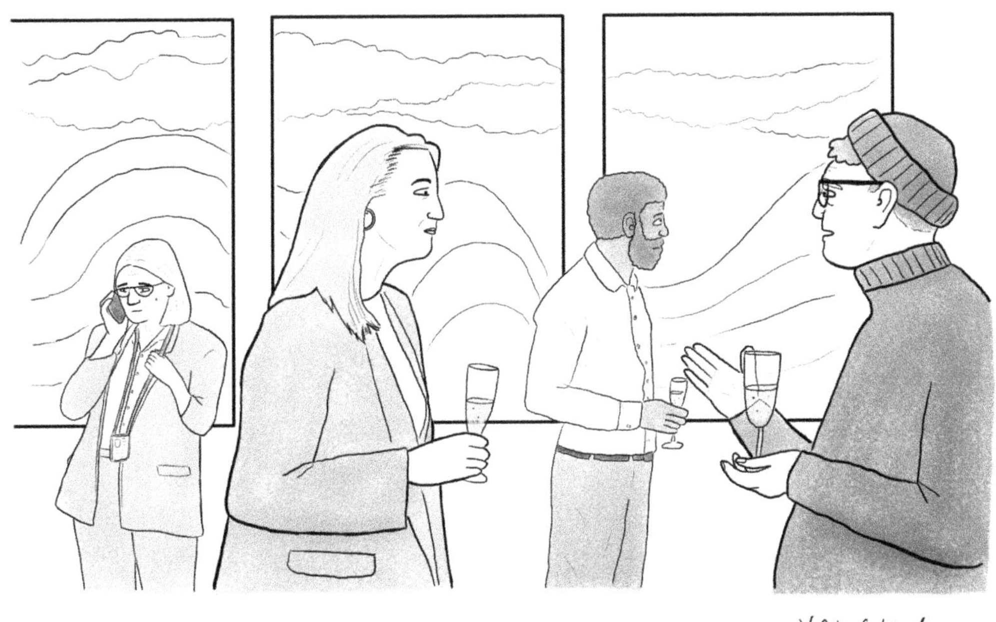

"AI could make the art, but tax evasion is a lot more fun when someone else is involved."

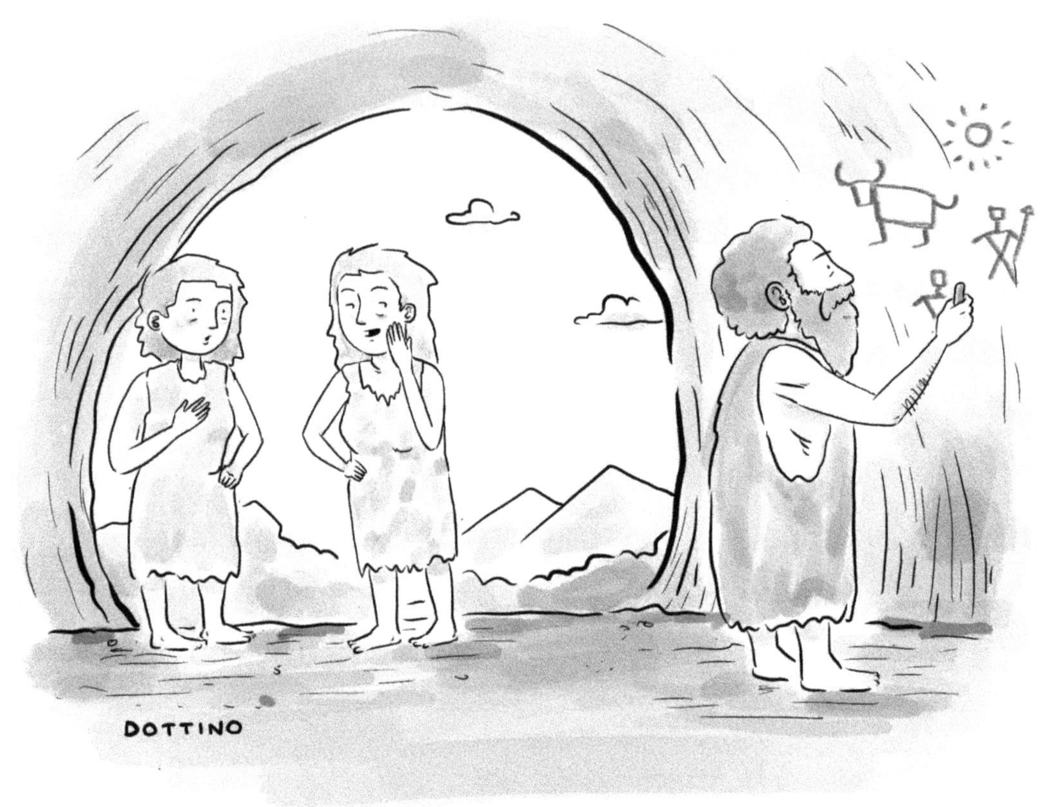

"Can you believe it? He's a hunter-gatherer ***and*** *artist."*

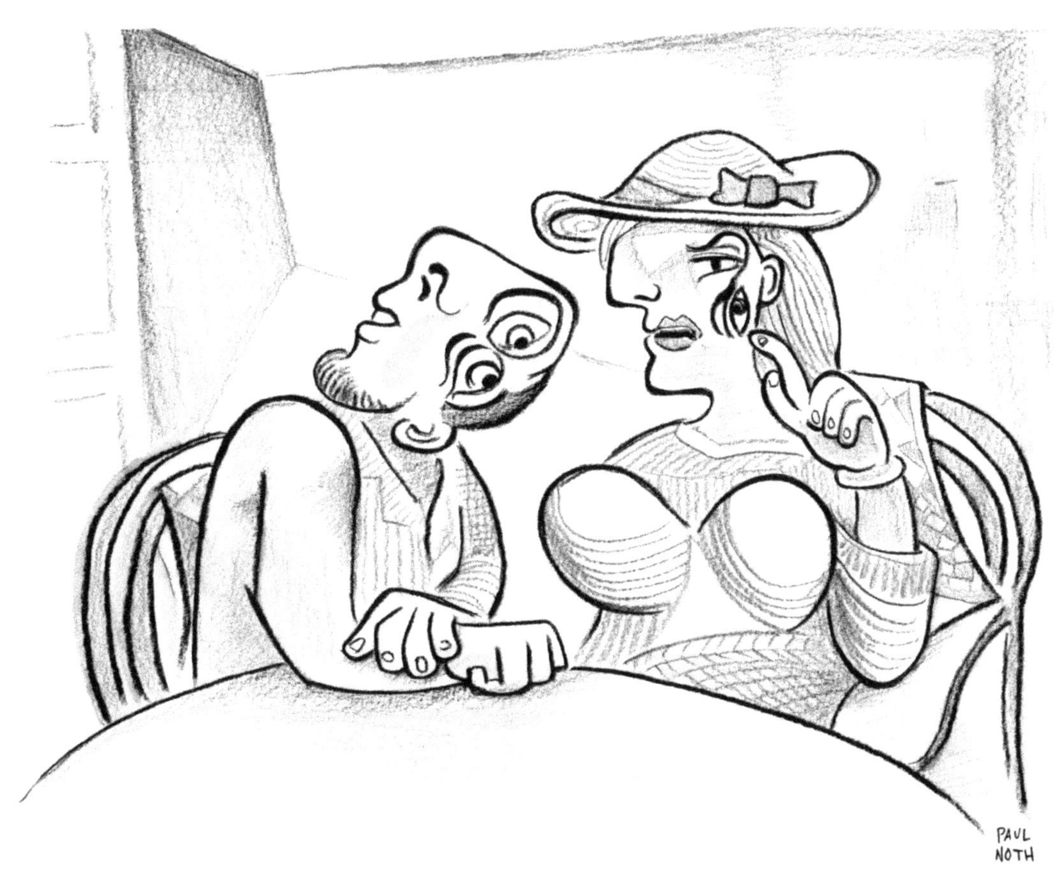

"Uh, hello? My eyes are over here."

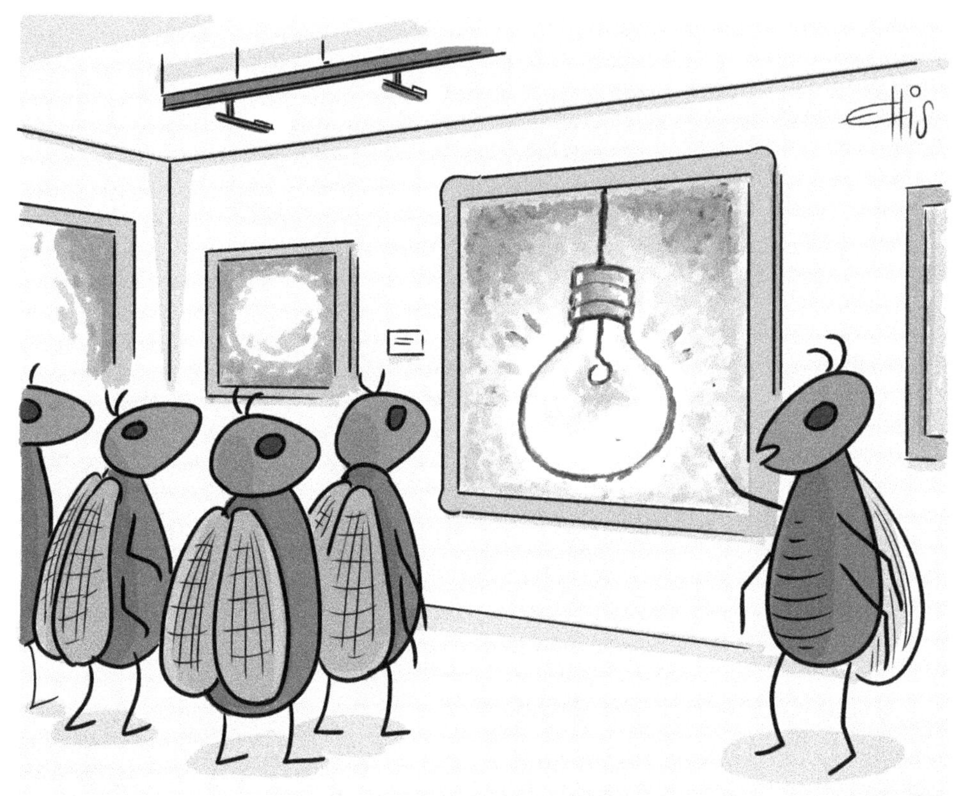

"Notice how the artist utilizes light to draw in the viewer."

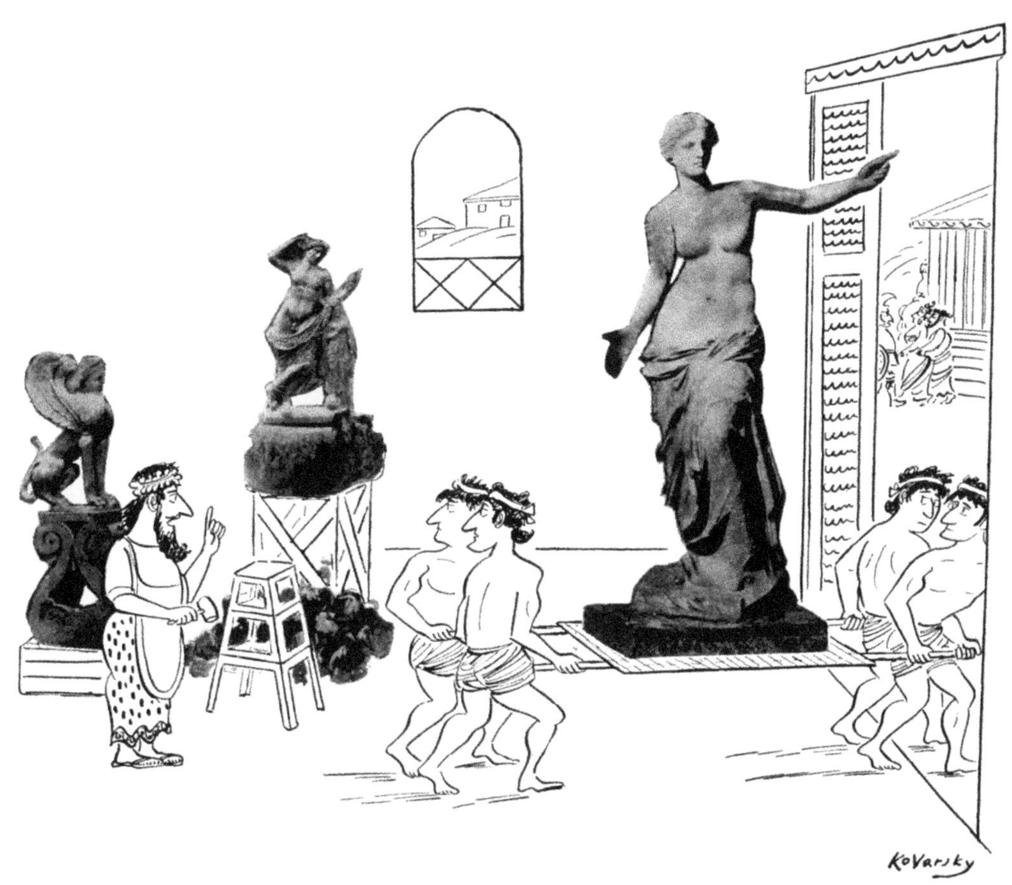

"Careful now. It's fragile."

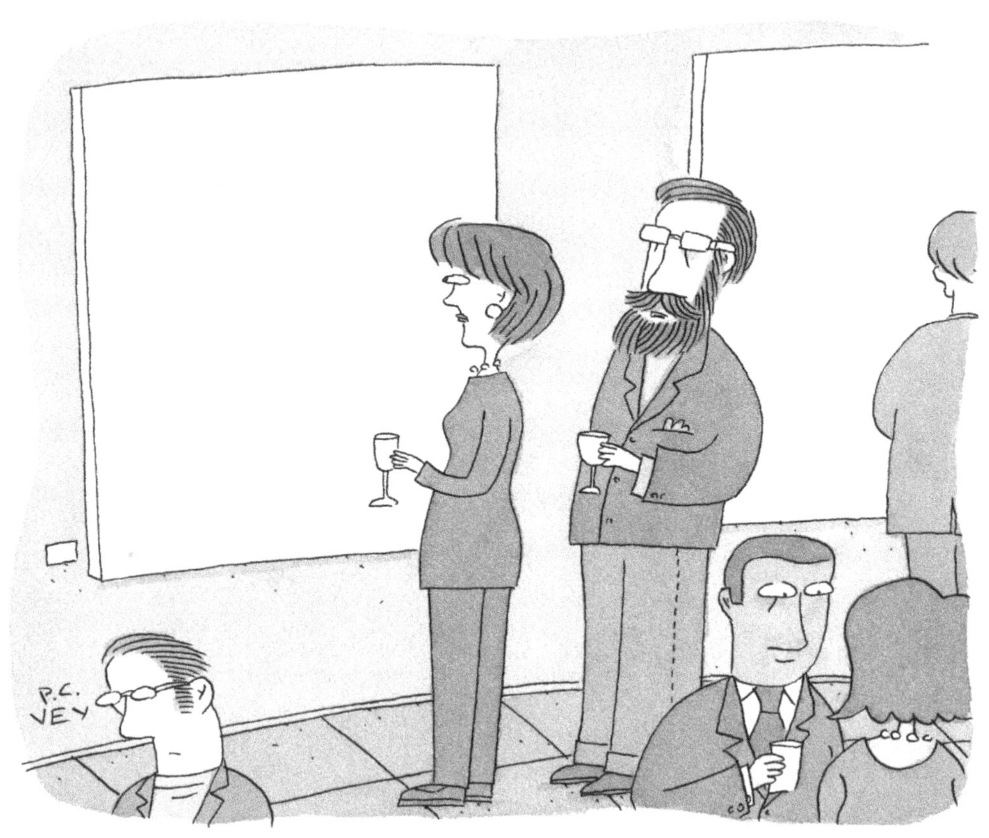

"I love the way the empty canvas saves on paint."

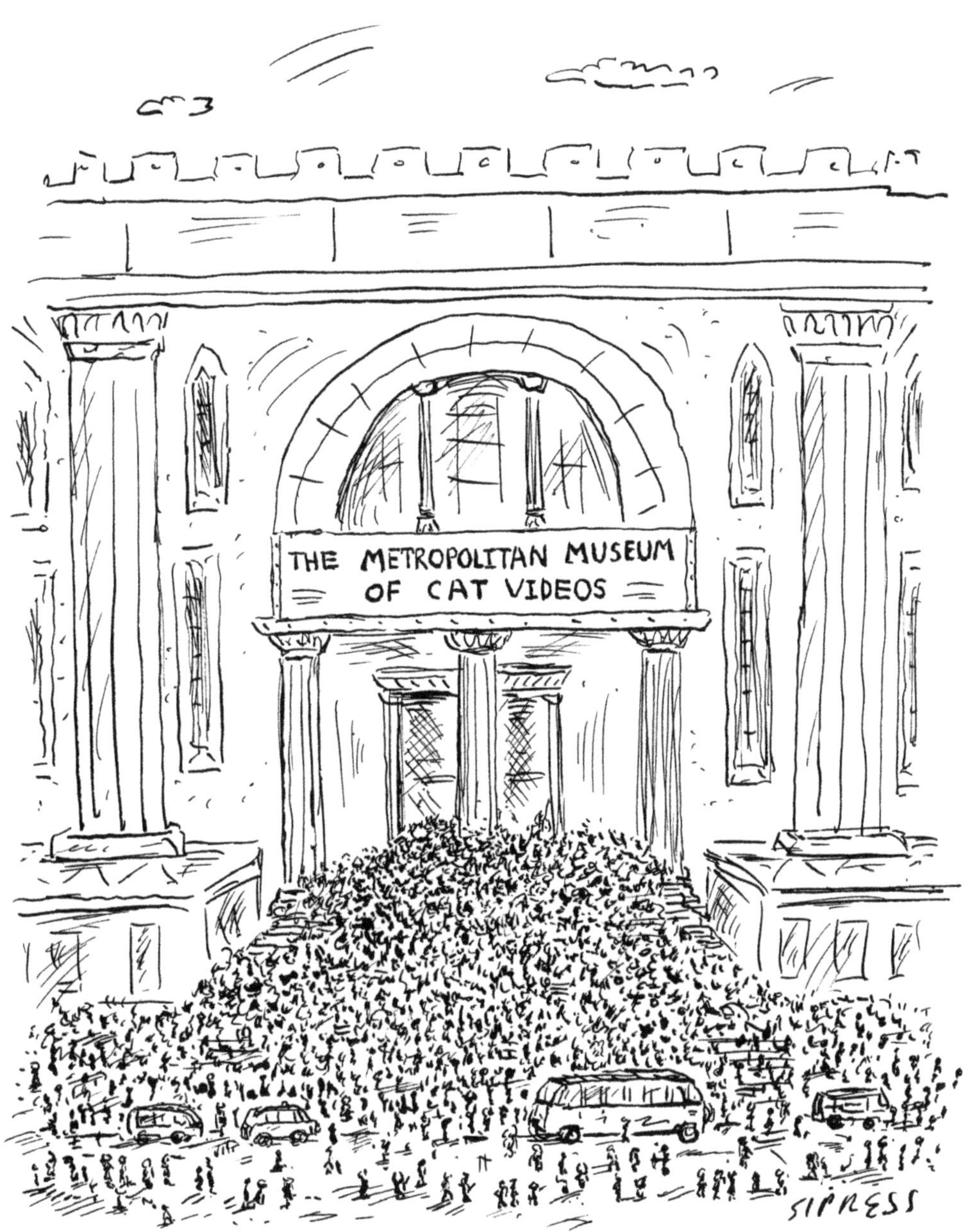
THE METROPOLITAN MUSEUM
OF CAT VIDEOS
SIPRESS

OTHER REMBRANDT MISATTRIBUTIONS

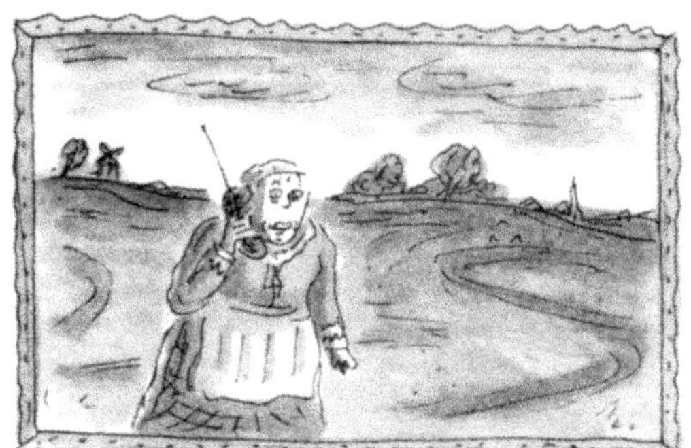
Old Woman with Cellular Phone

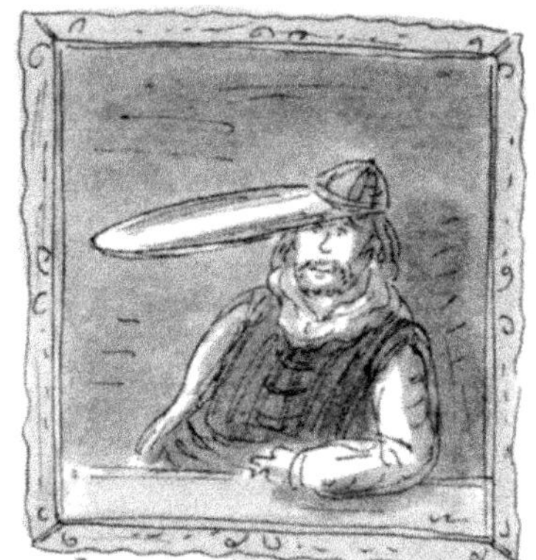
Self-Portrait in Oversized-Brim Baseball Cap

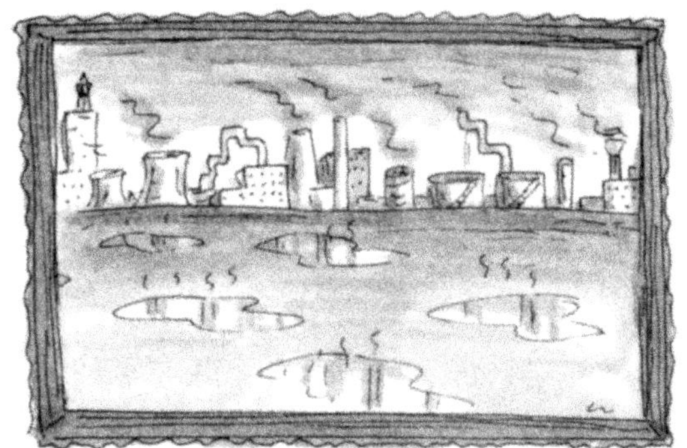
View of Rotterdam

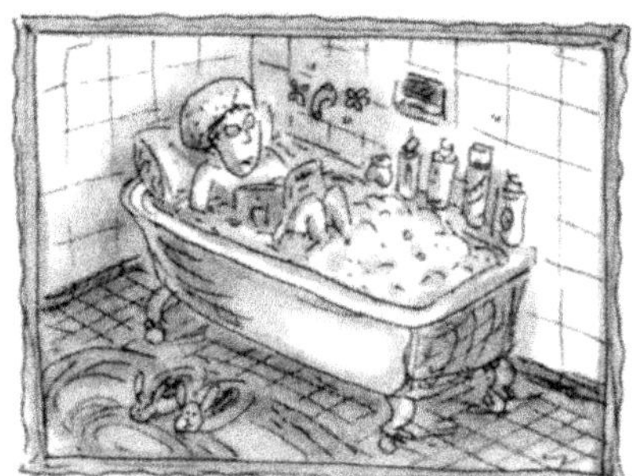
Young Girl at Her Bath

R. Chast

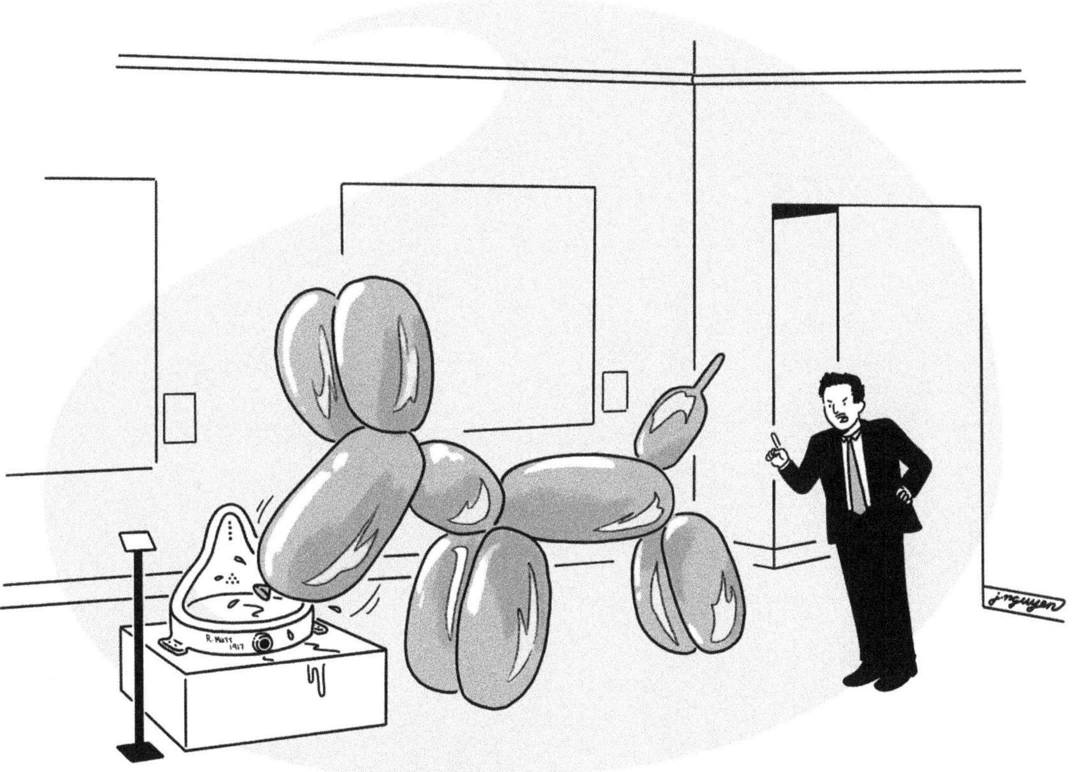

"Bad art! Bad!"

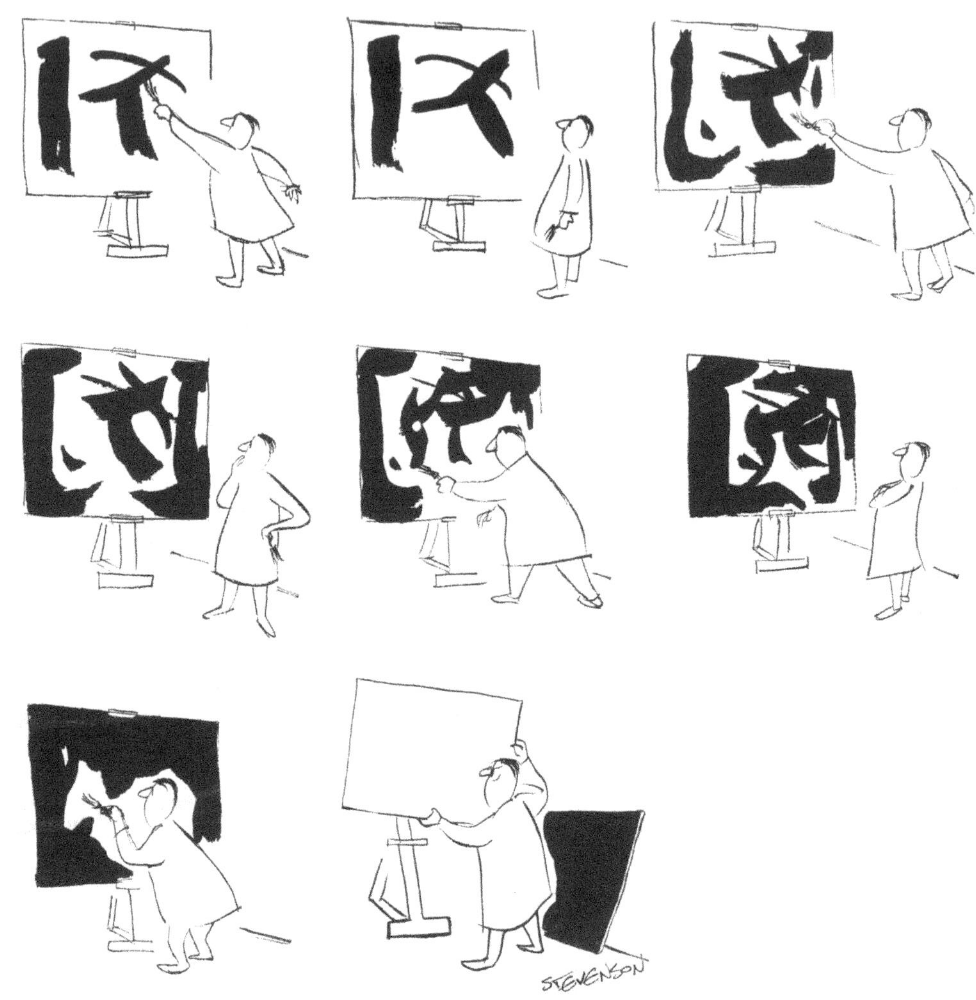
STEVENSON

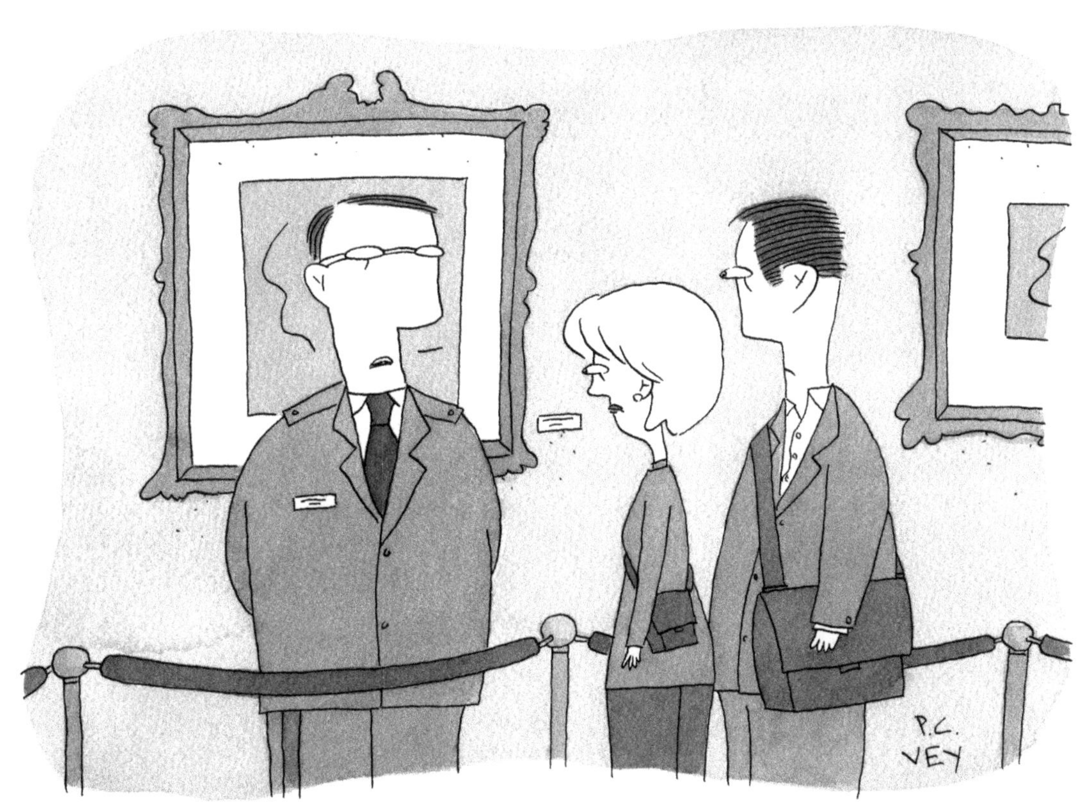

"For a better look at the painting, go to our Web site."

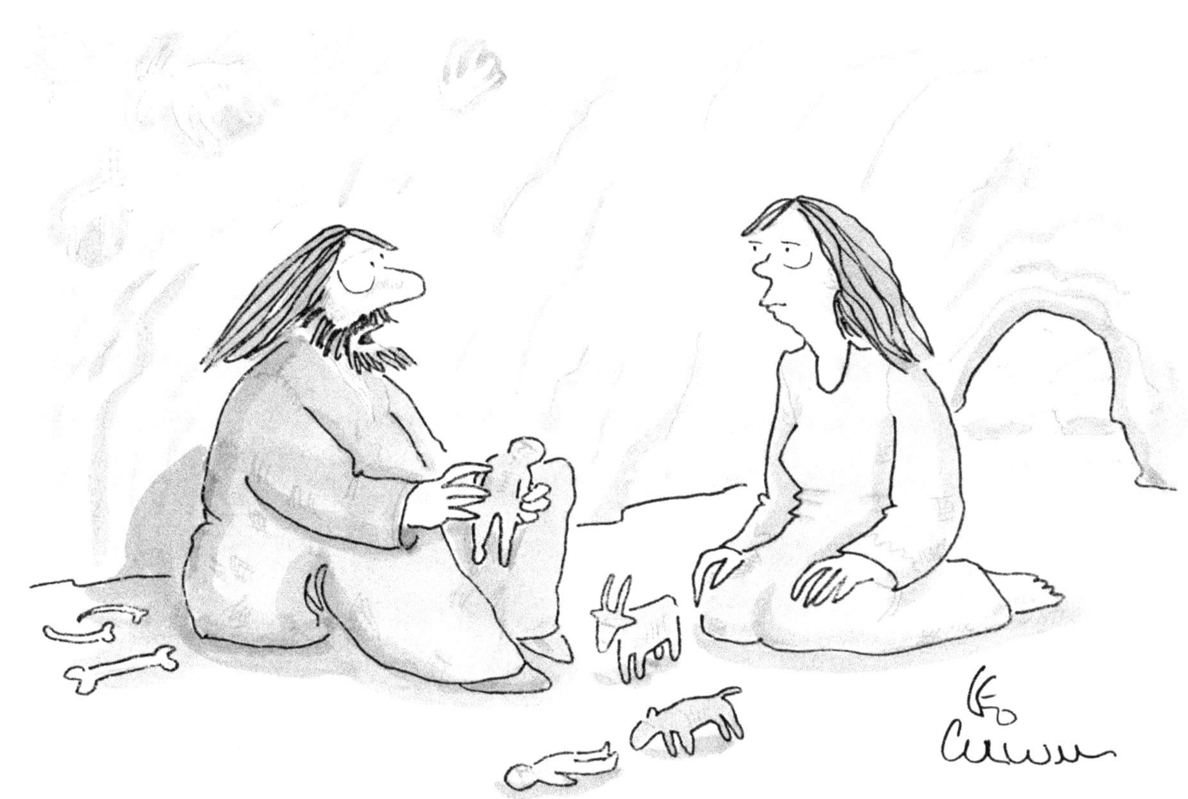

"Cave painting is dead. I'm into Claymation."

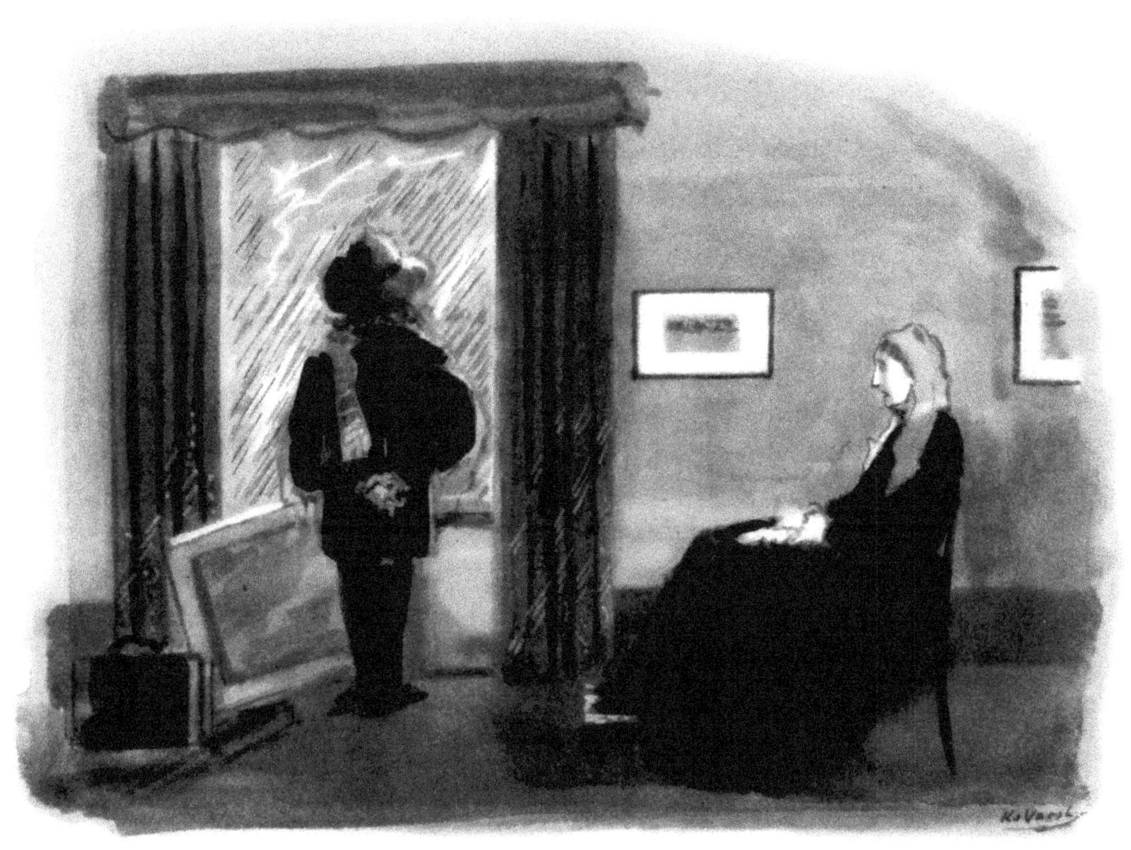

"Surely, Son, you can find something to paint indoors."

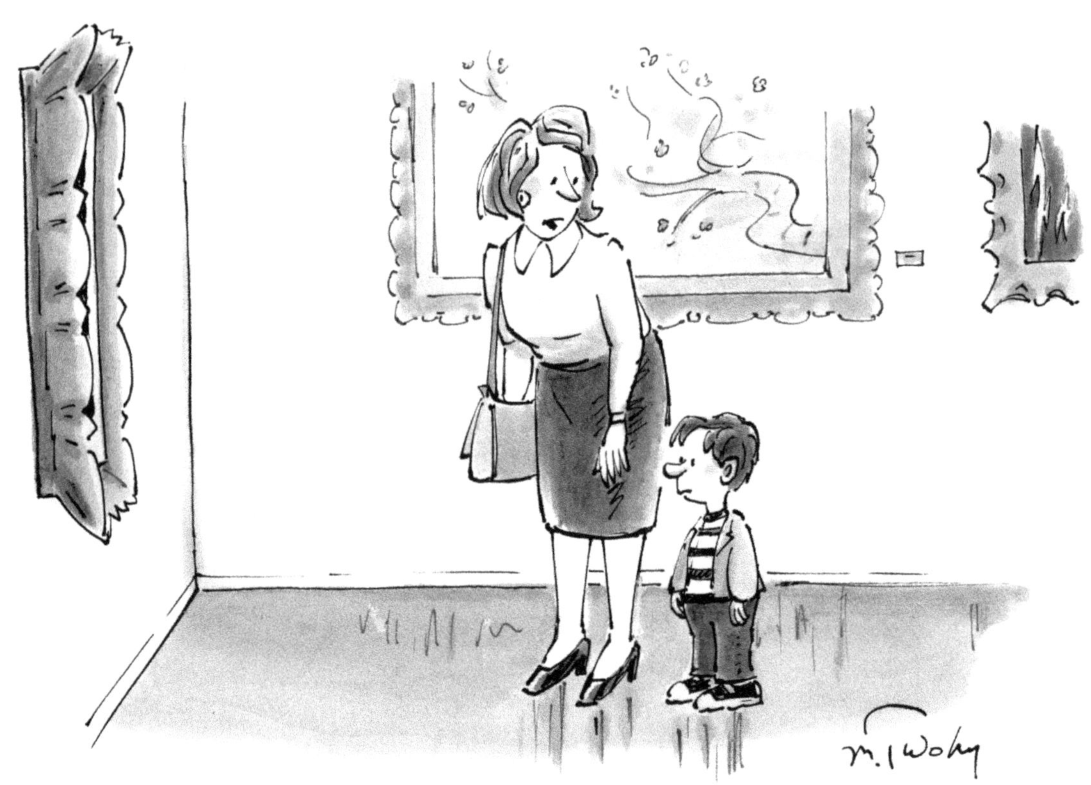

"Instead of 'It sucks' you should say, 'It doesn't speak to me'."

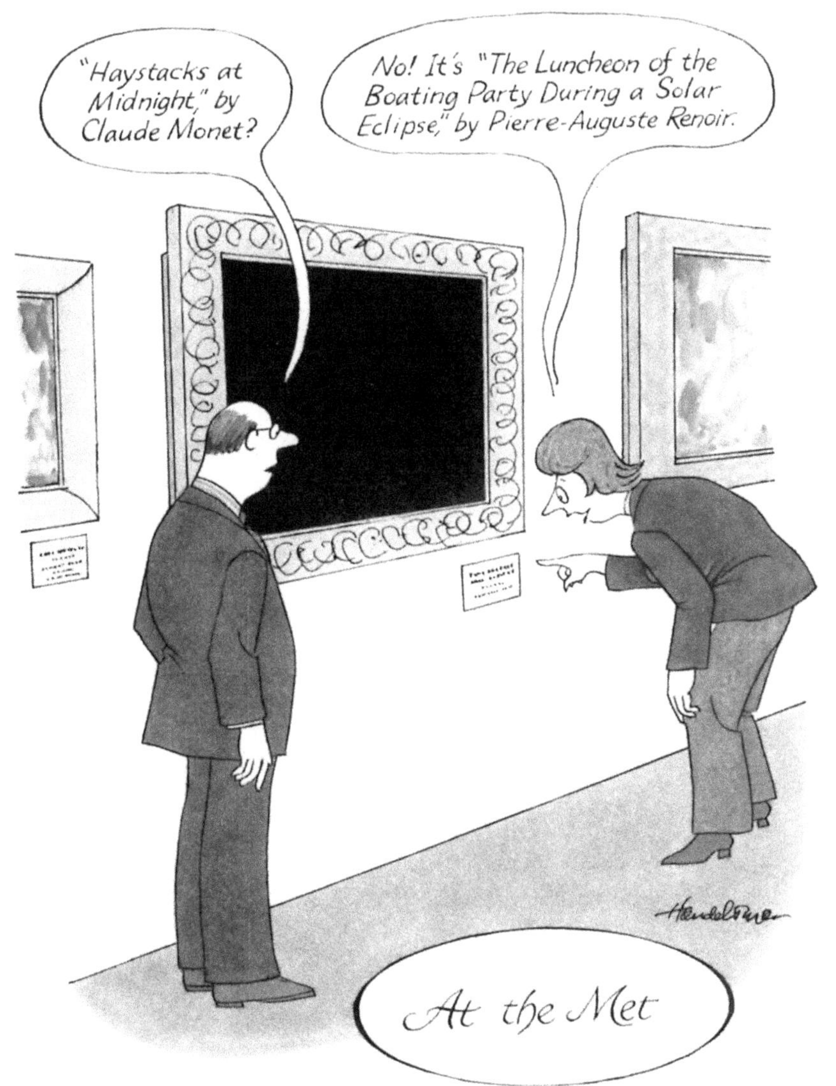
"Haystacks at Midnight," by Claude Monet?
No! It's "The Luncheon of the Boating Party During a Solar Eclipse," by Pierre-Auguste Renoir.
At the Met

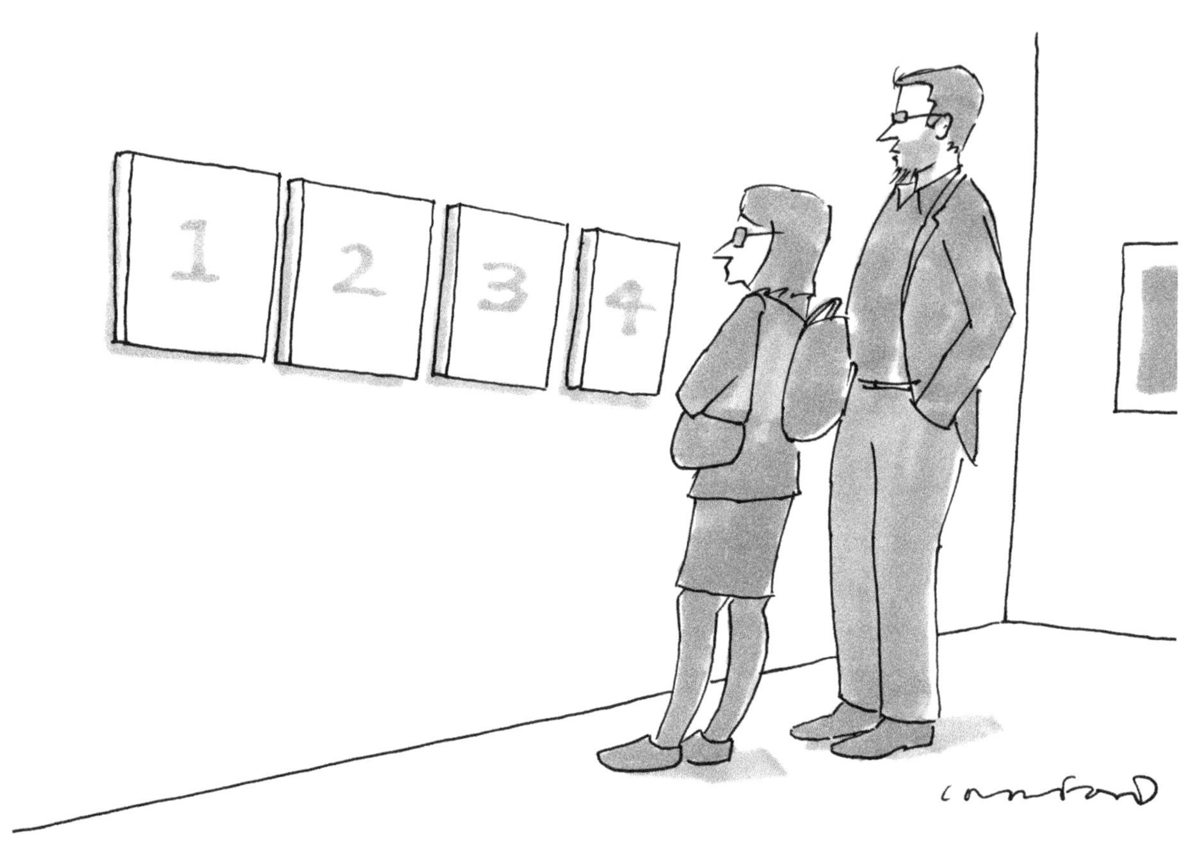

"'3' is genius. We need to buy '3'."

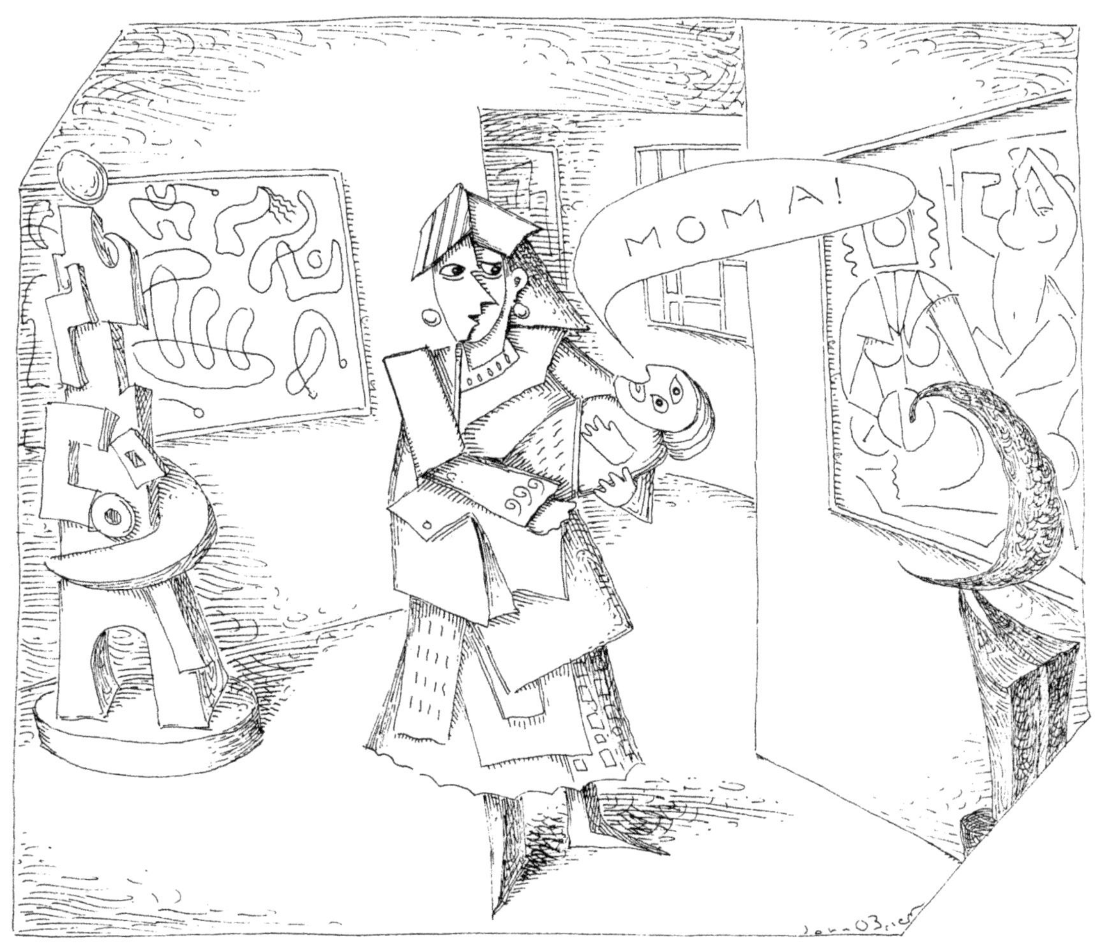
MOMA!

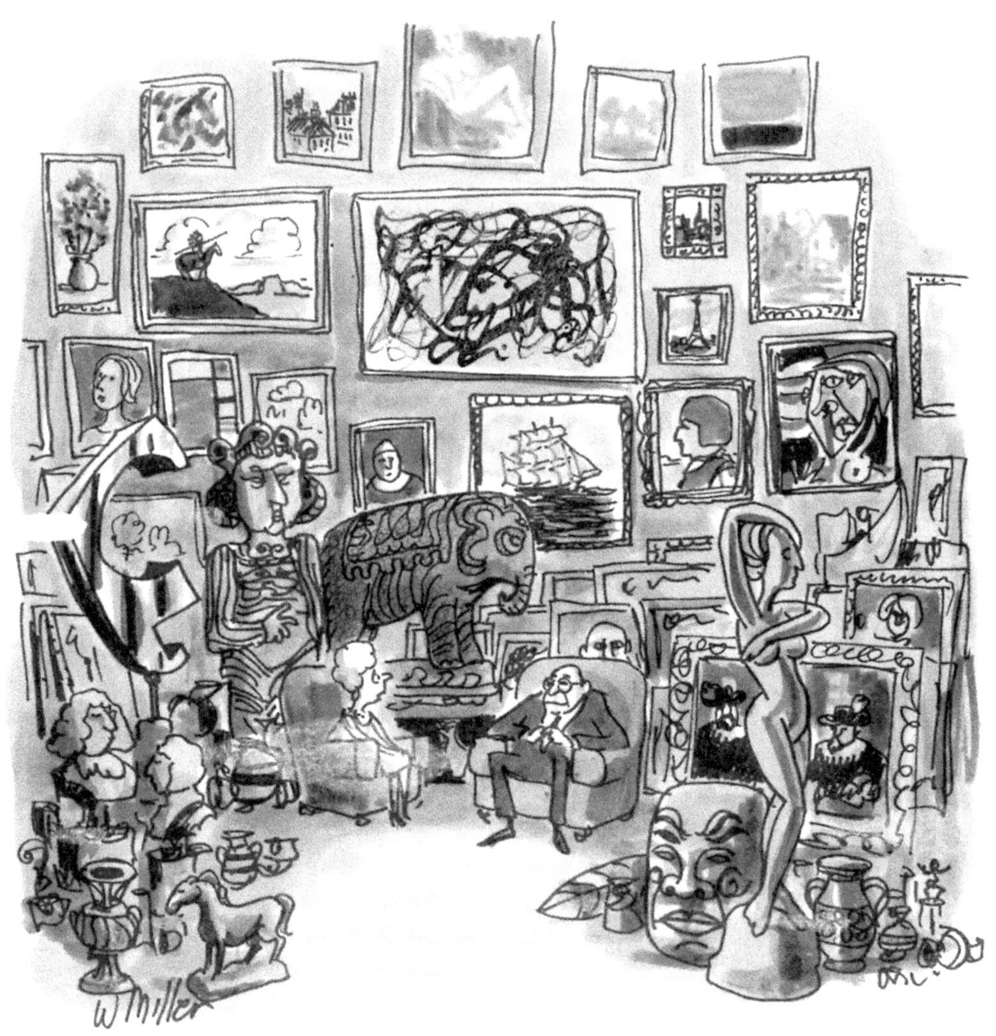

"Edgar, don't you think it's time you donated a wing somewhere?"

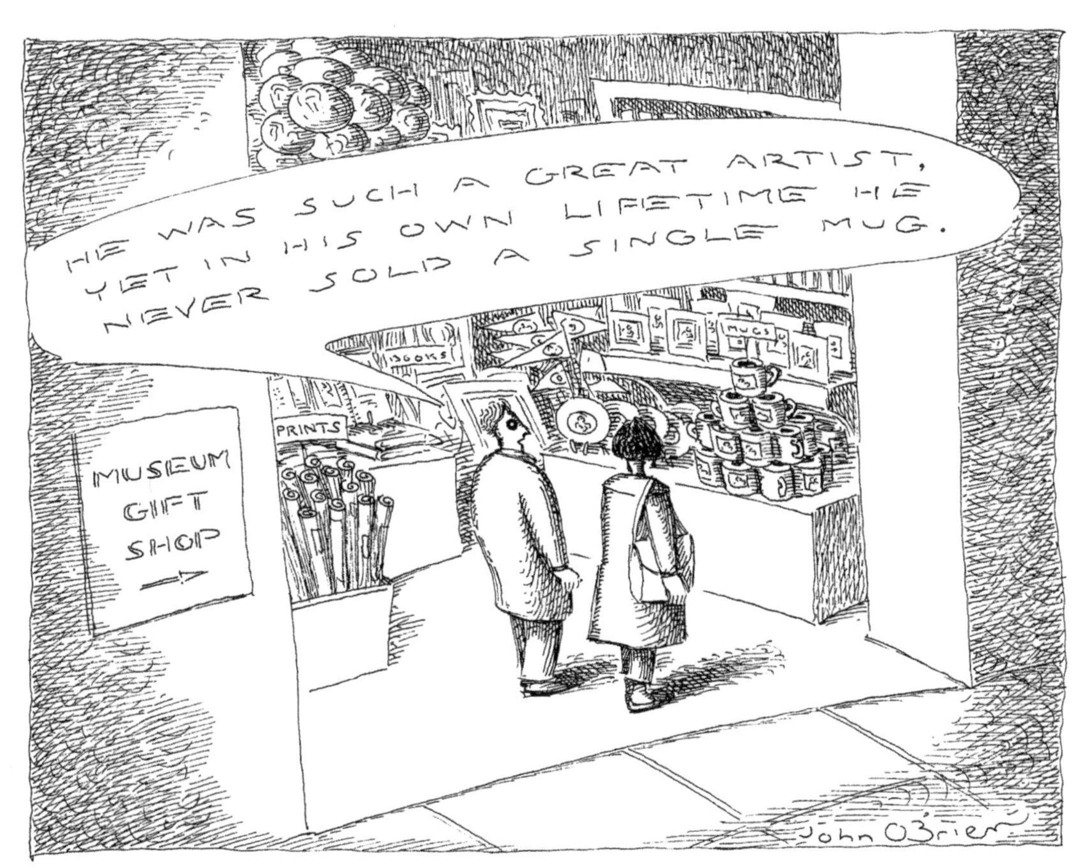
HE WAS SUCH A GREAT ARTIST, YET IN HIS OWN LIFETIME HE NEVER SOLD A SINGLE MUG.
MUSEUM GIFT SHOP
PRINTS
BOOKS
MUGS
John O'Brien

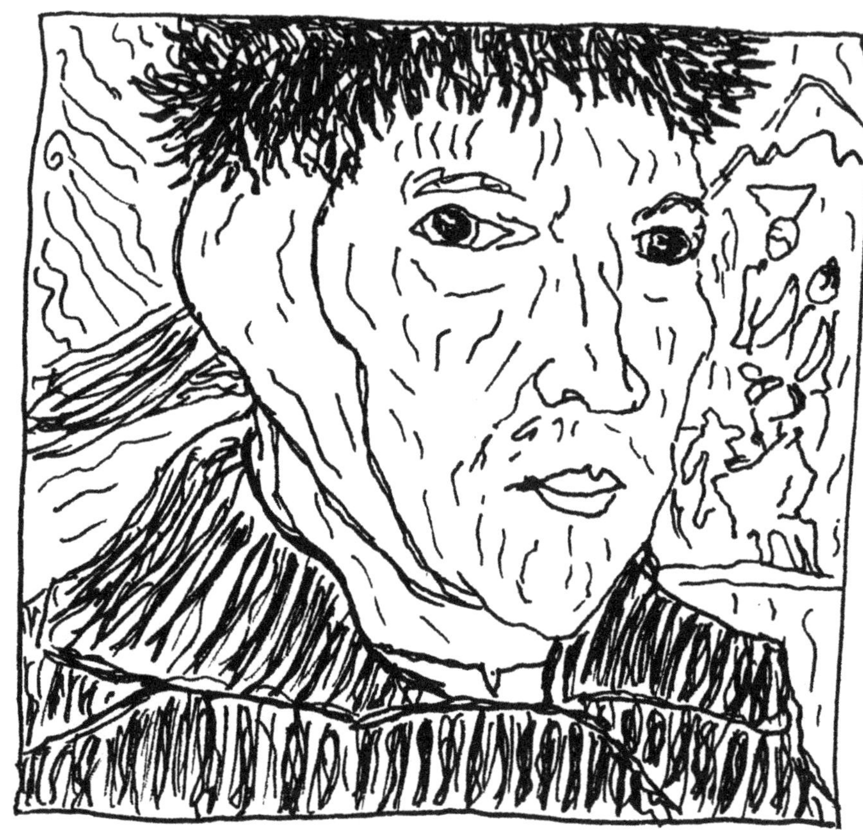

Liked by theovangogh

vvg #earcutoff #lunaticasylum #cantgoon #rejection #noonegetsme #depthsofhell #help #badheadache #broke

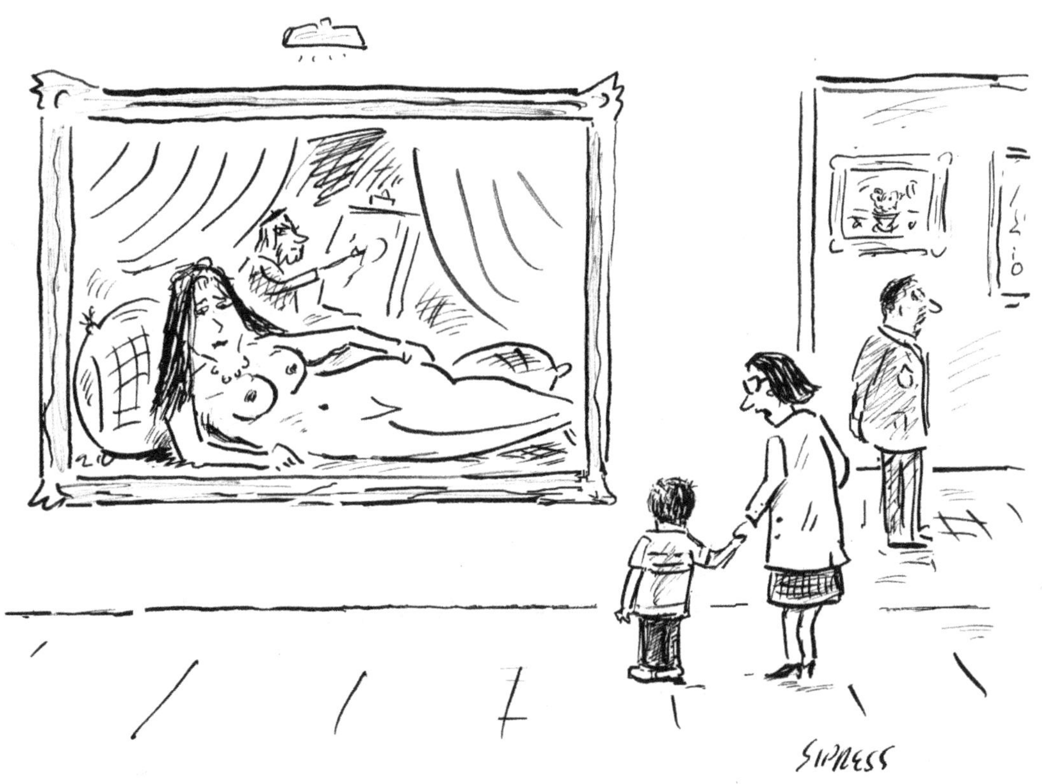

"If it's in a museum, you're allowed to look."

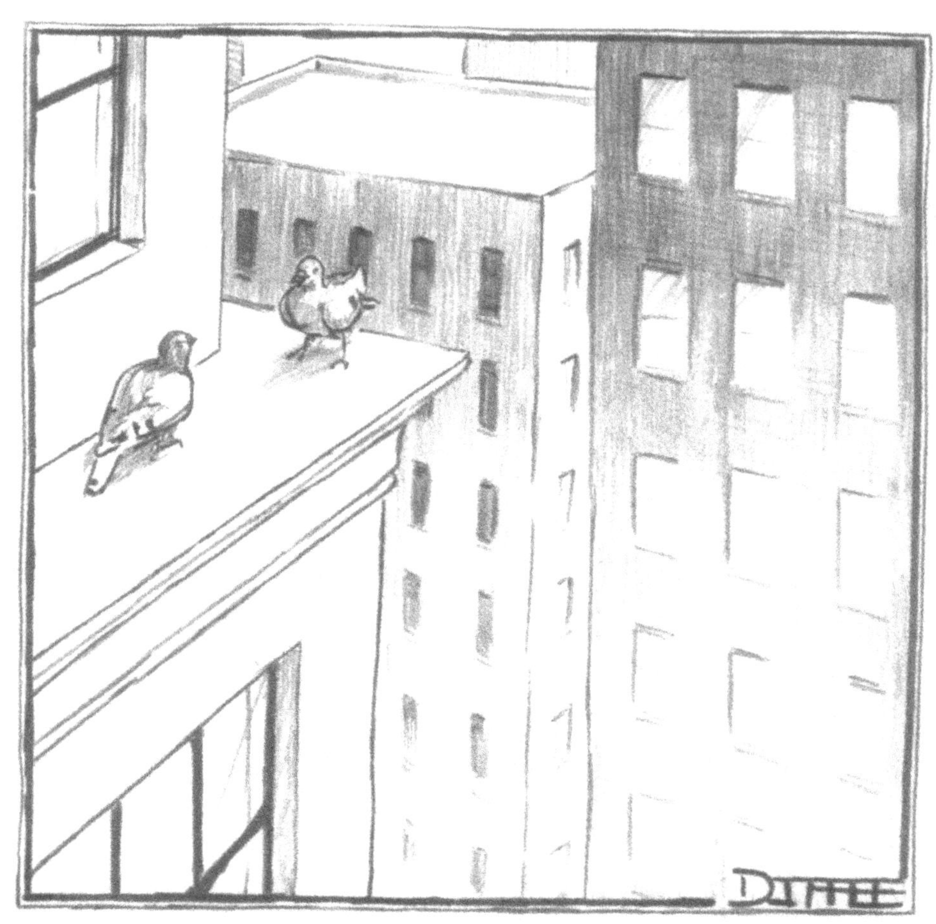

"I'd say my biggest influence is probably Pollock."

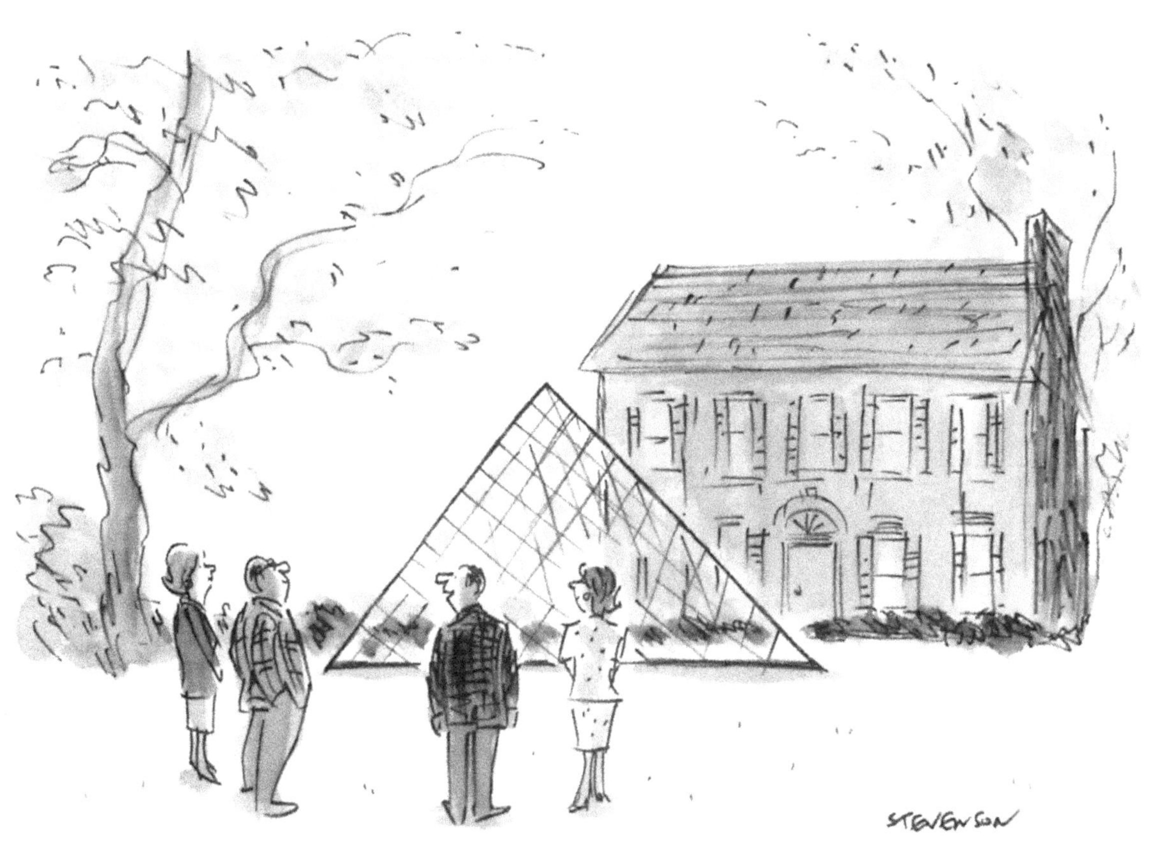

"Quite frankly, we stole the idea from I. M. Pei."

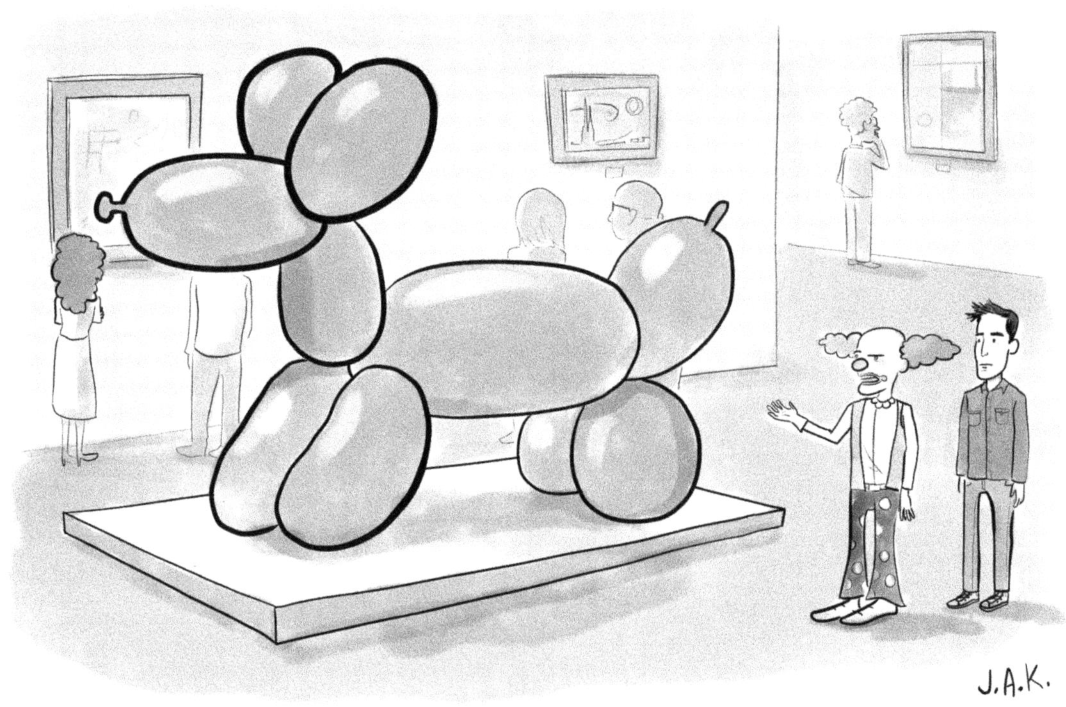

"I could do that."

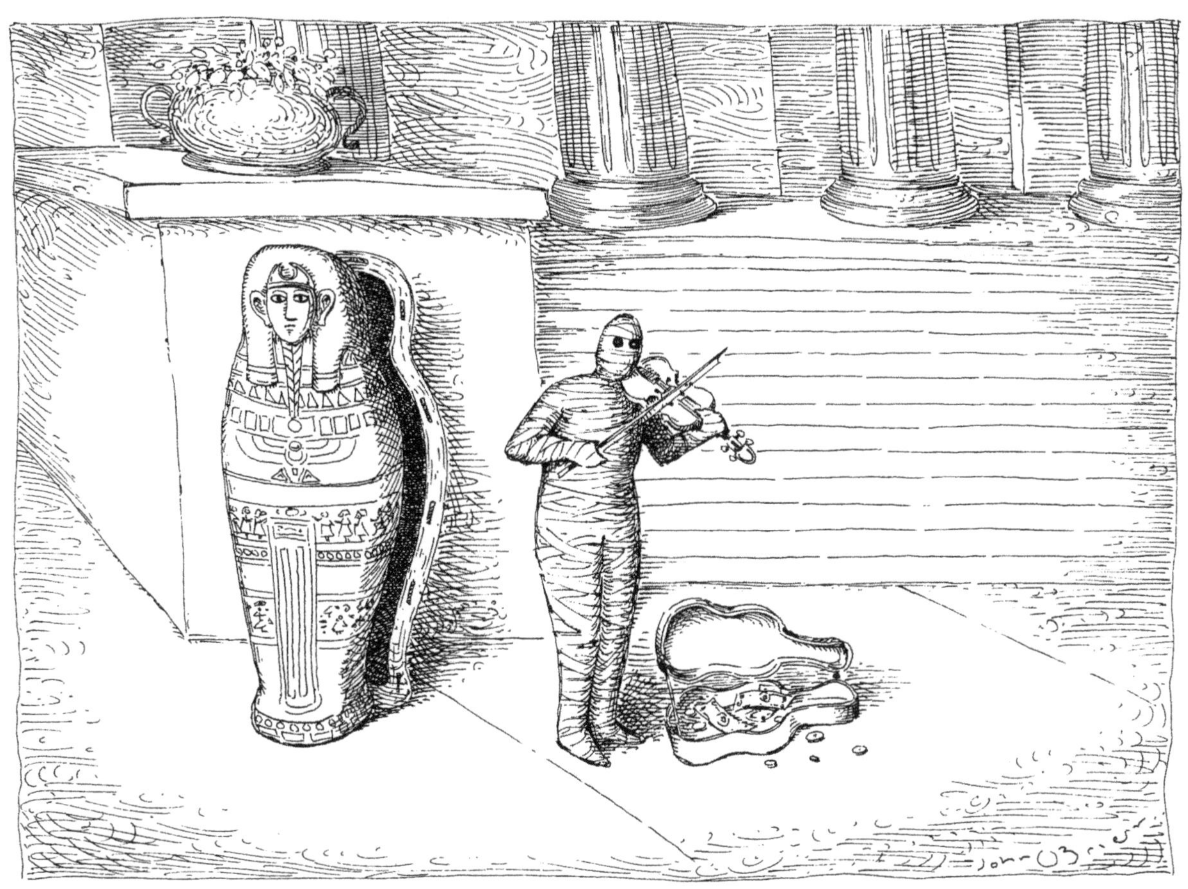

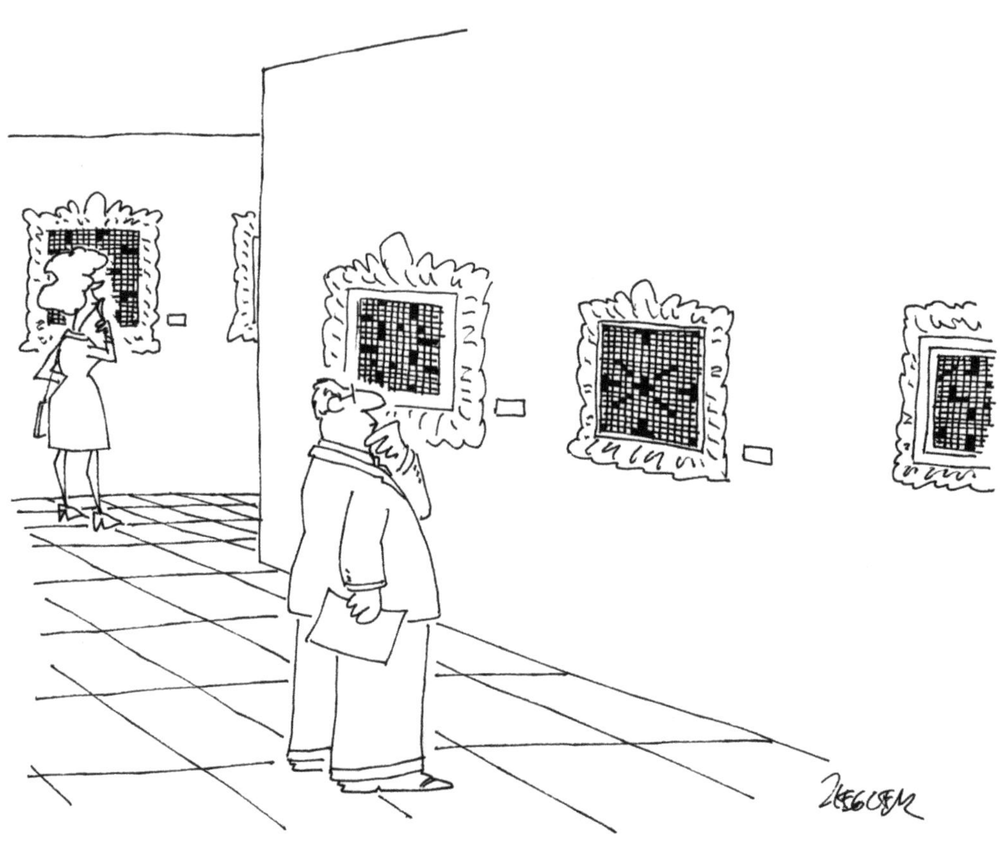

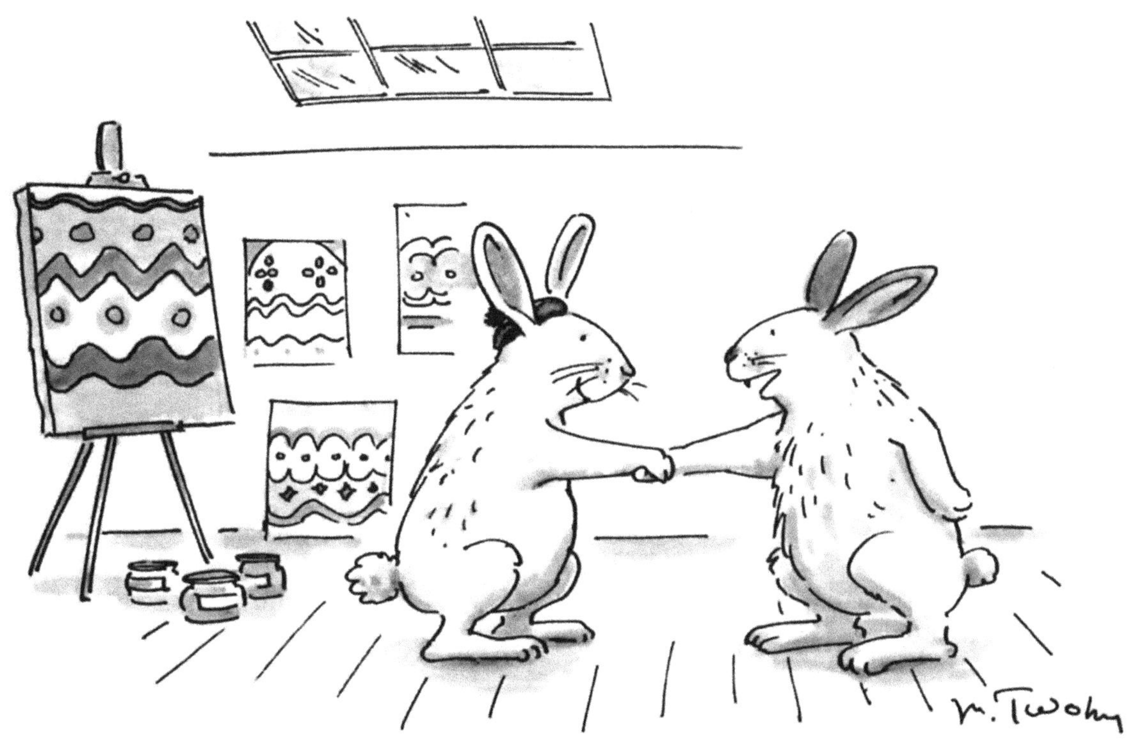

"I hear you've been doing exciting things with eggs and dye."

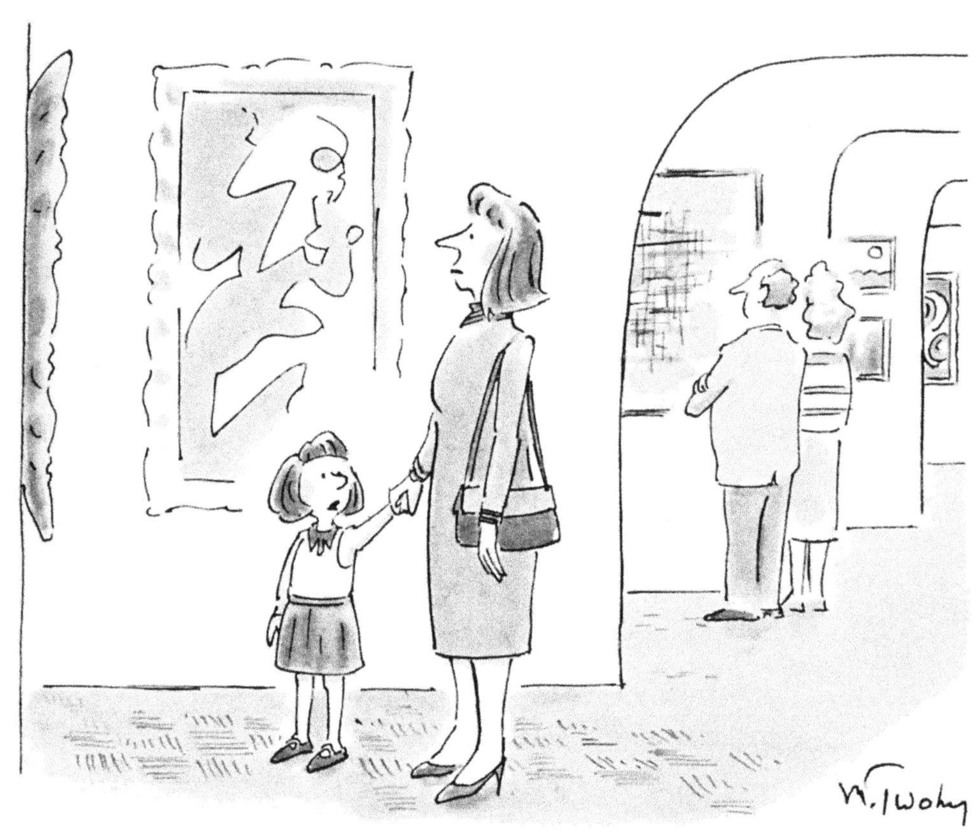

"Now can we have an eating experience?"

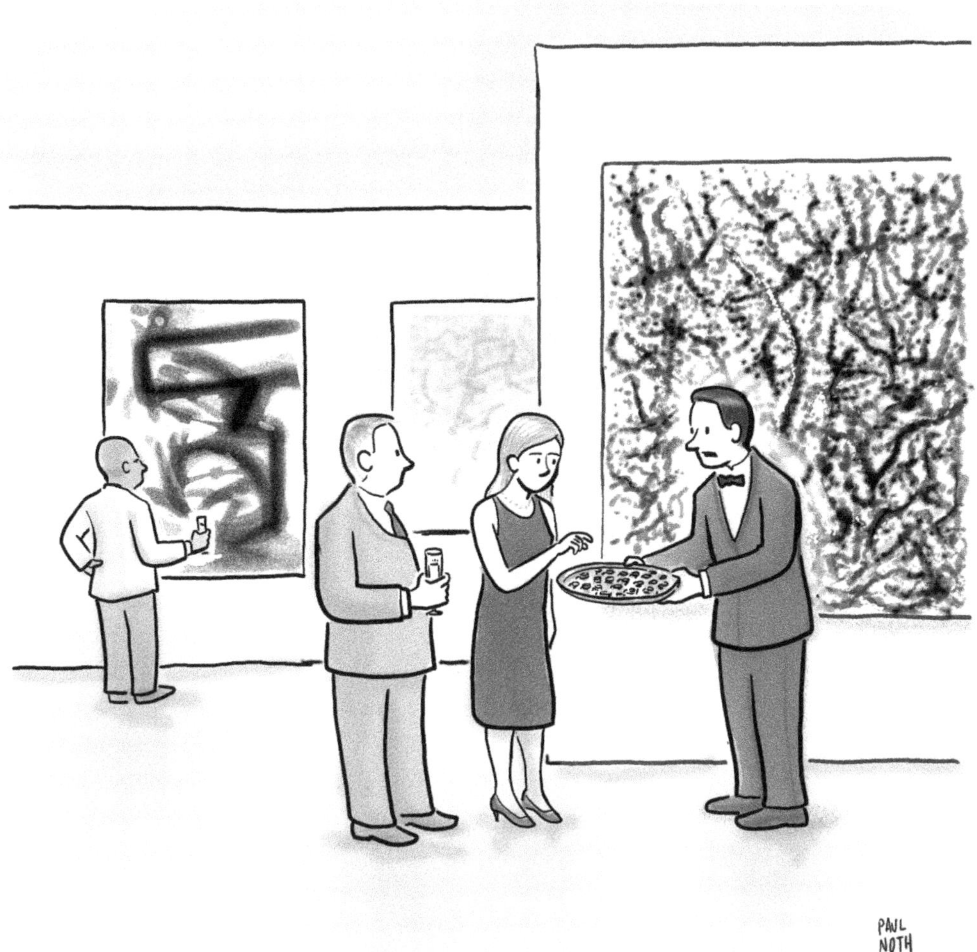

"The pink ones are sashimi, and I believe the little yellow ones just fell off the Pollock."

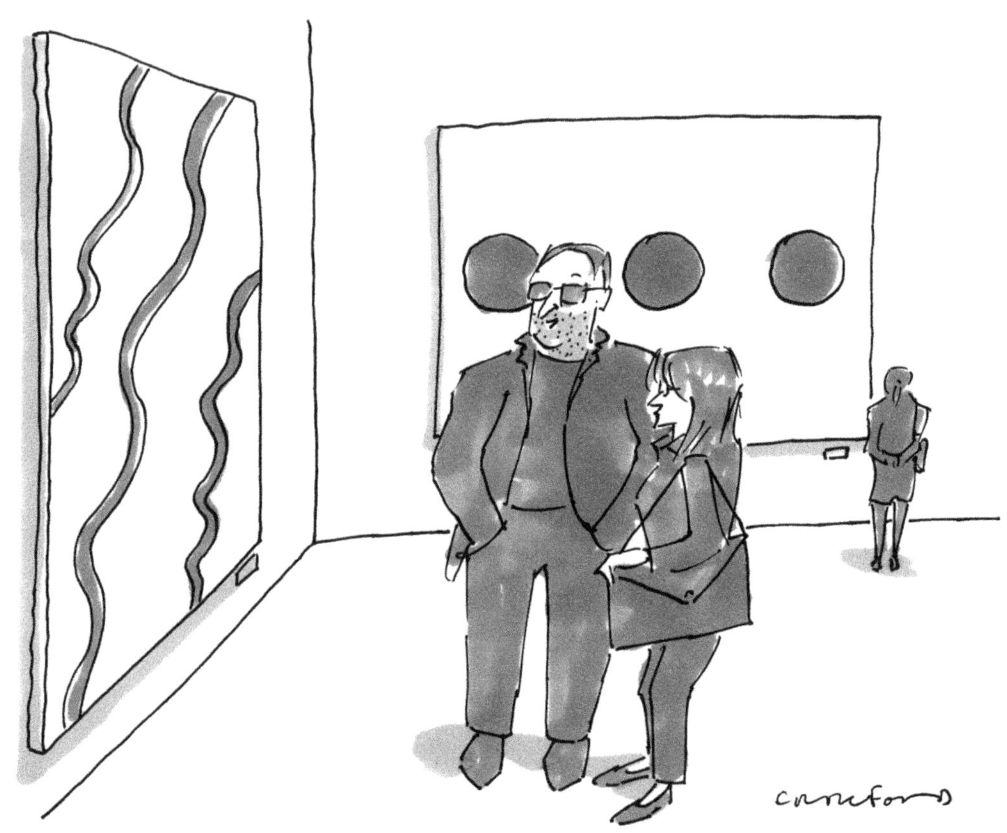

"It's meaningless, lady, believe me—I painted it."

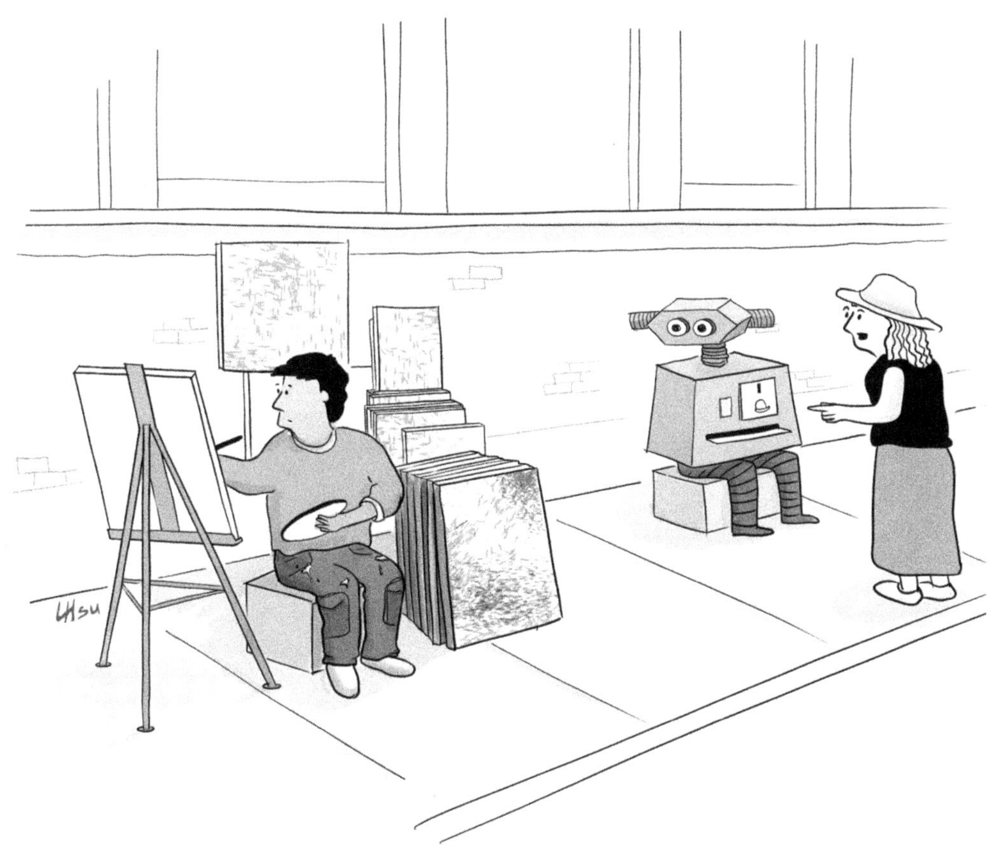

"I'd like a portrait of me in the style of him."

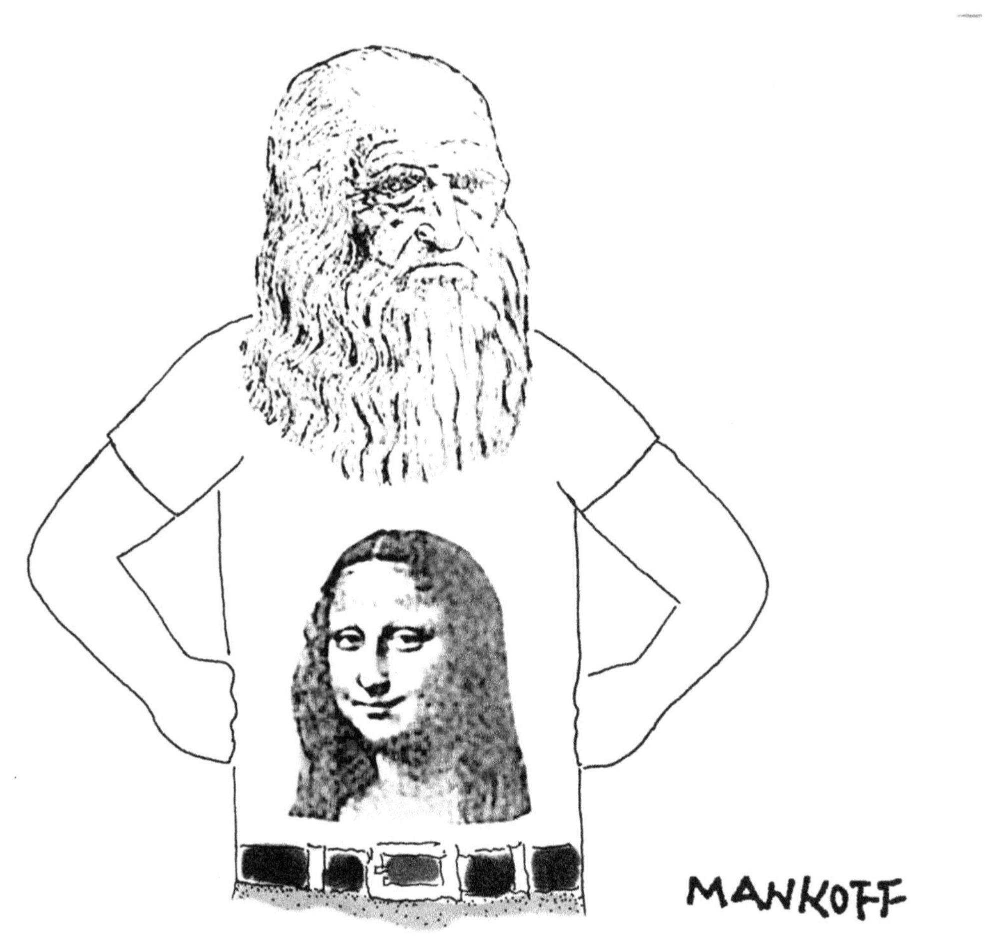
MANKOFF

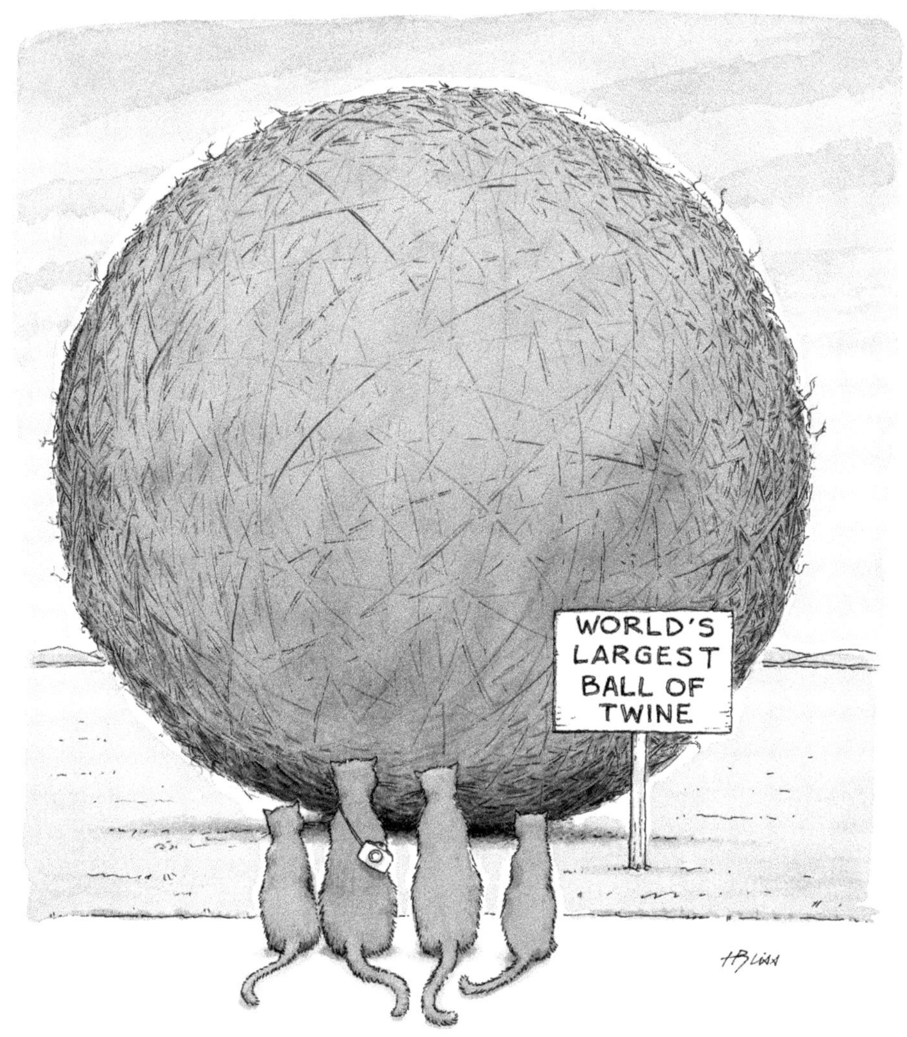
WORLD'S
LARGEST
BALL OF
TWINE

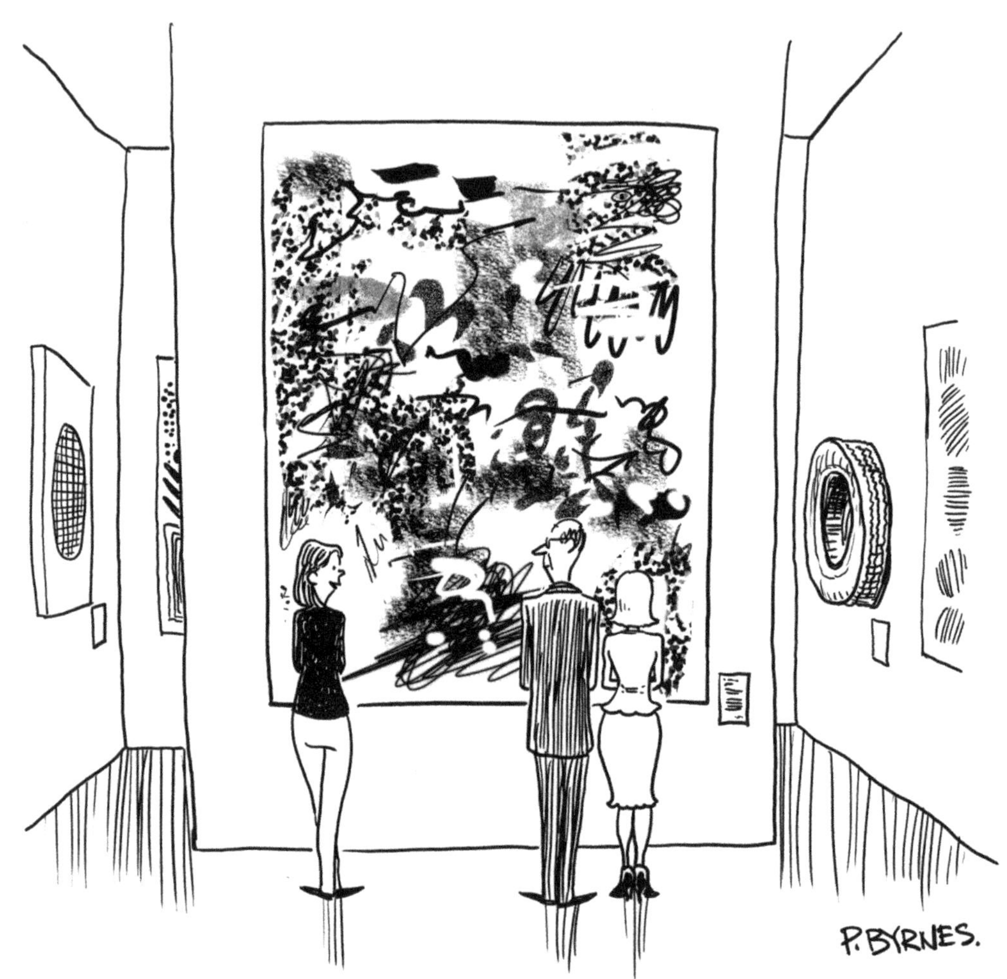

"My two-year-old actually did paint that."

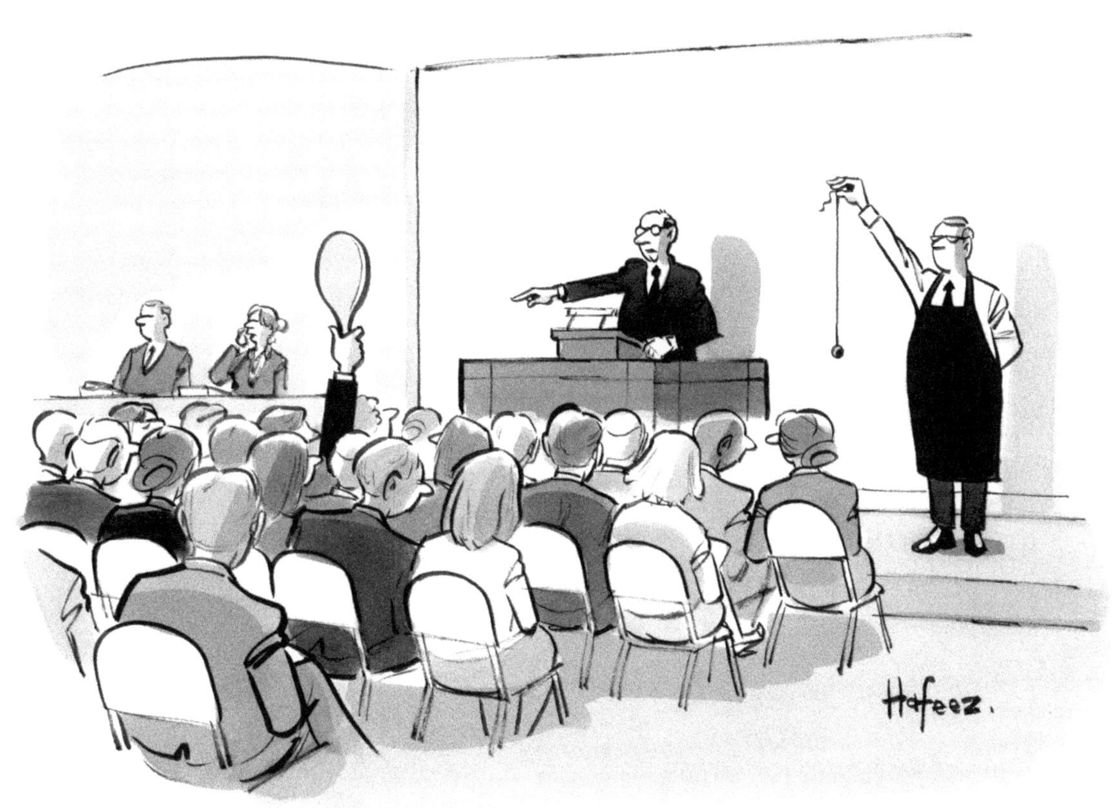

"Sold, to the gentleman with the paddle."

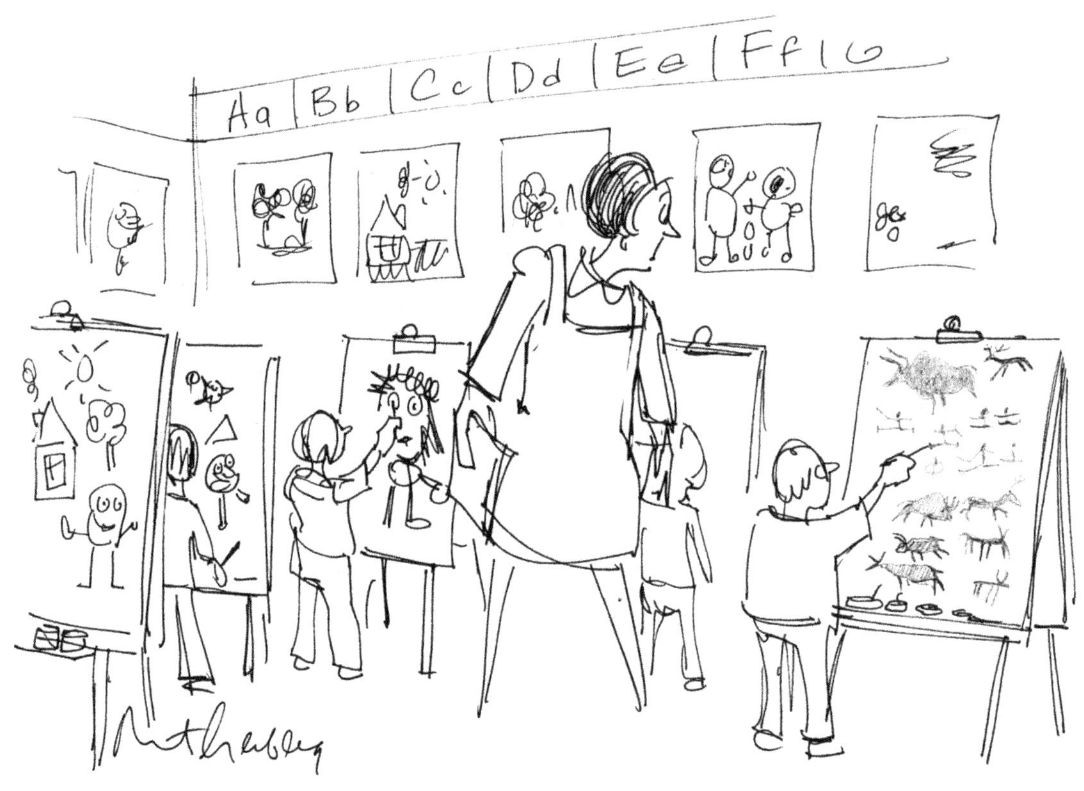
Aa | Bb | Cc | Dd | Ee | Ff | G

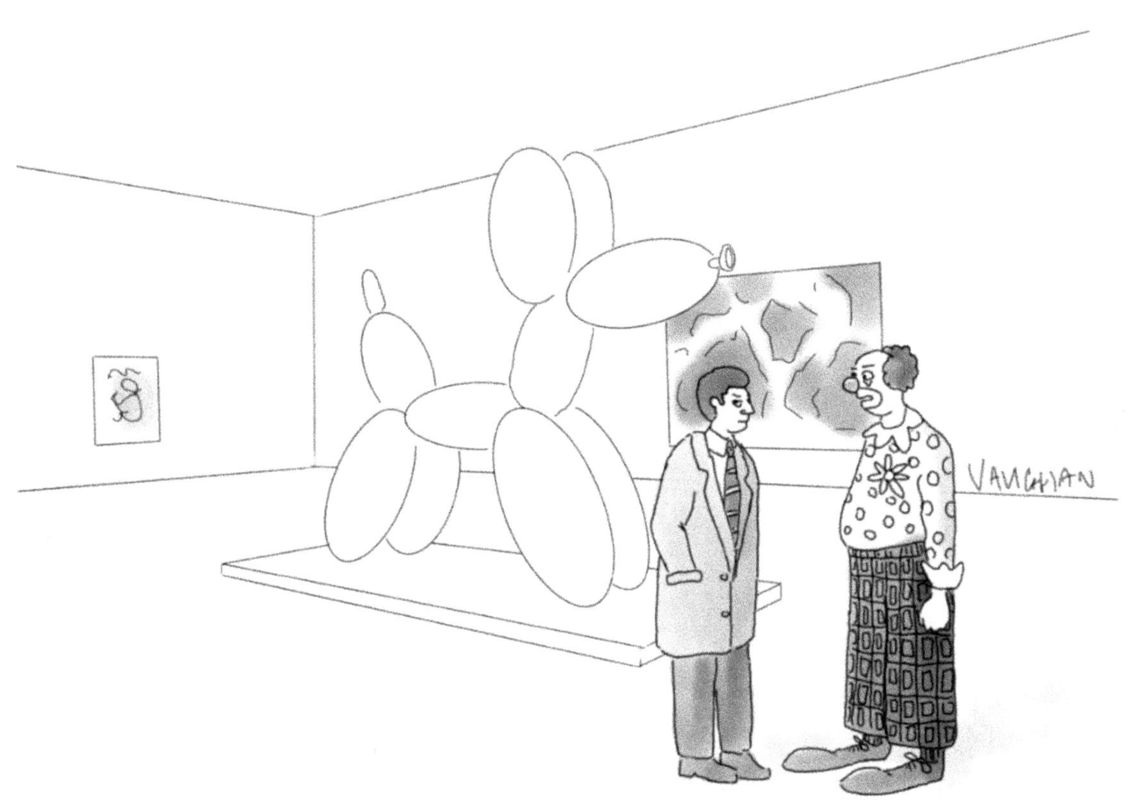

"Well, no, I wouldn't expect you to get it."

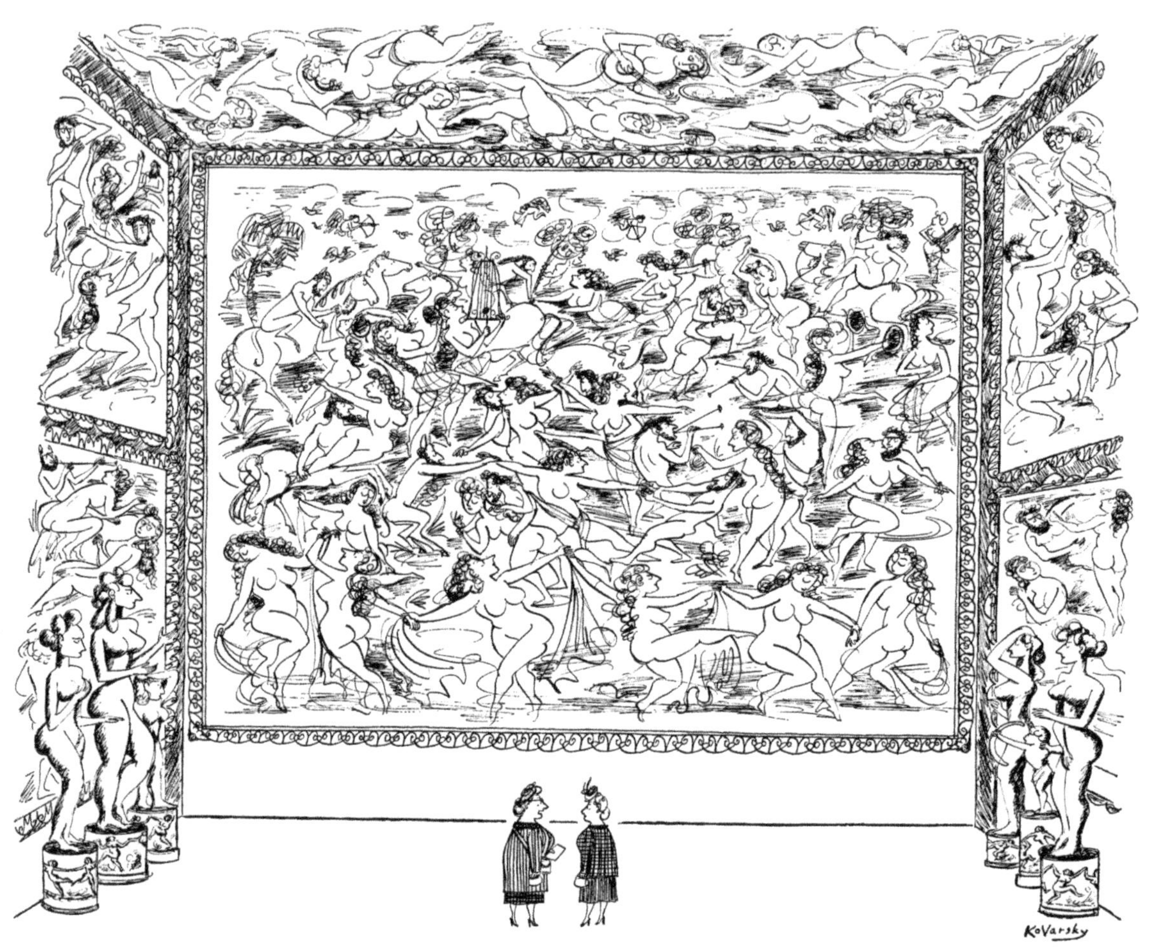

"Well, it's no wonder those Borgias and Medicis were always poisoning each other."

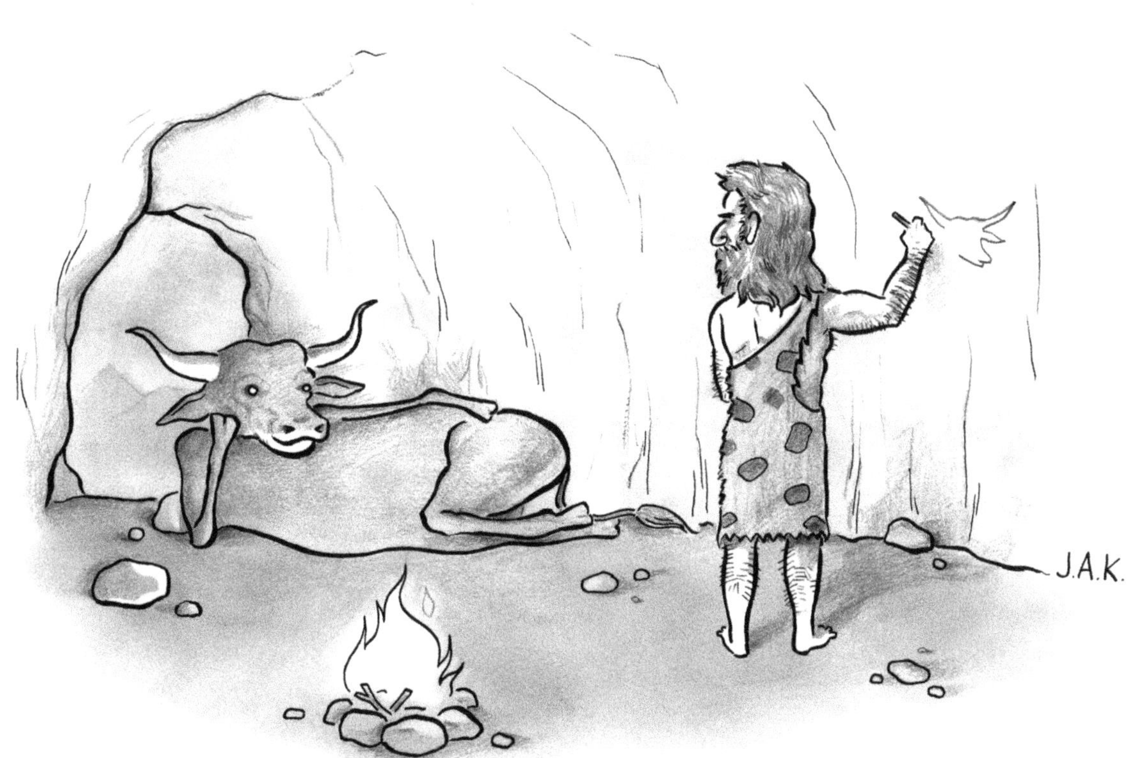
J.A.K.

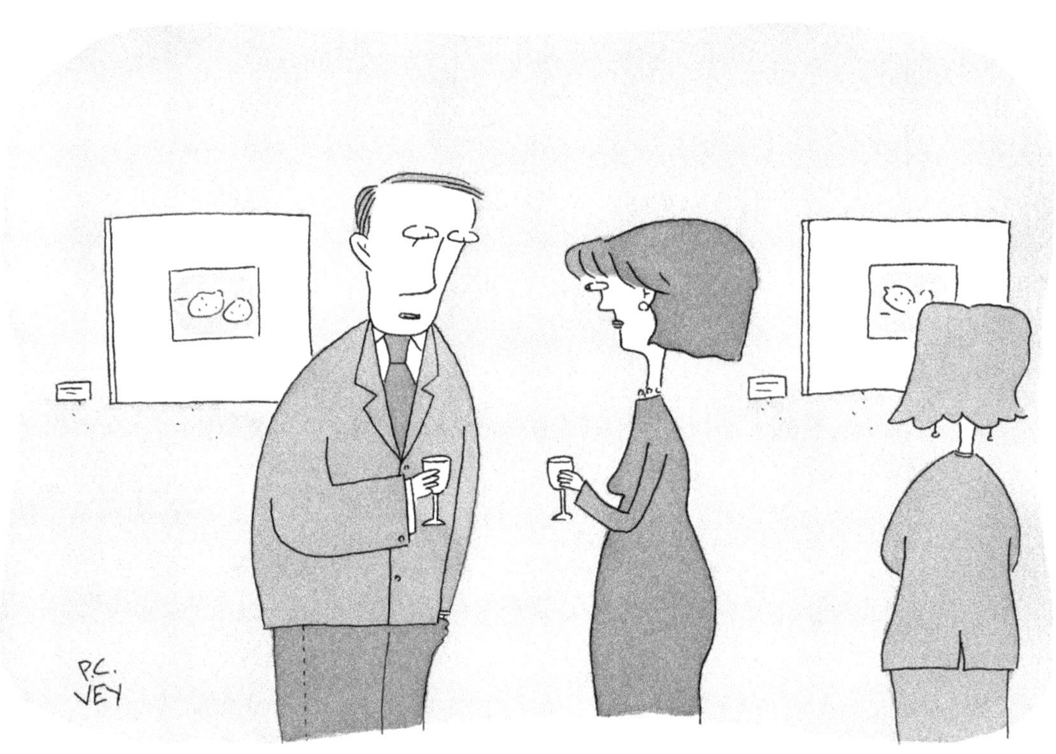

"If life gives you lemons, photograph them and produce small edition affordable prints."

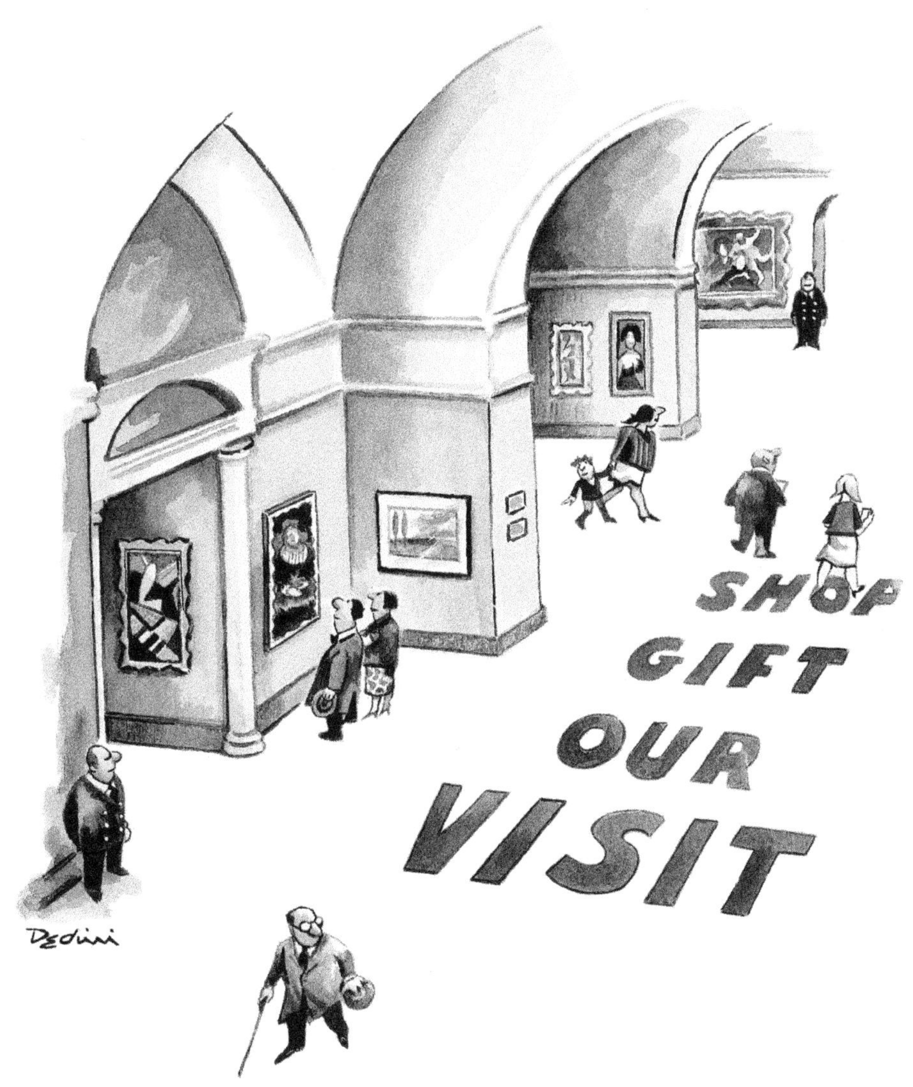
VISIT
OUR
GIFT
SHOP
Dedini

IN PRIVATE COLLECTIONS

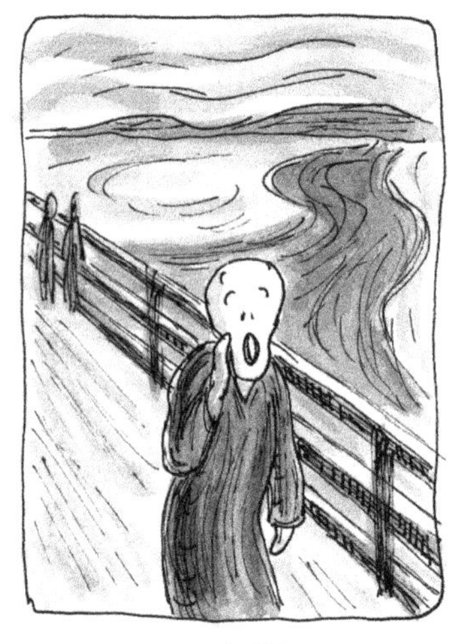

THE YAWN

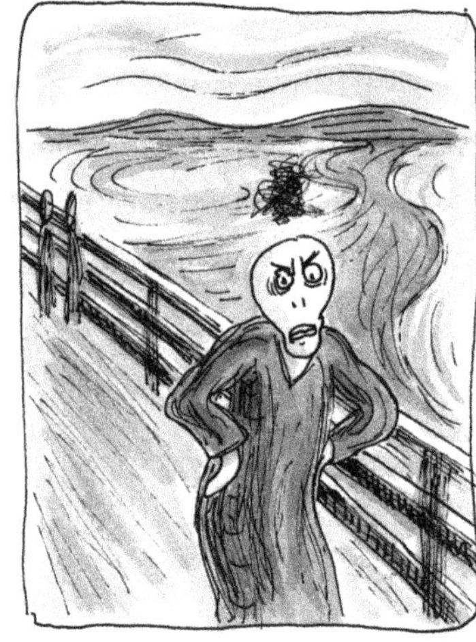

THE POUT

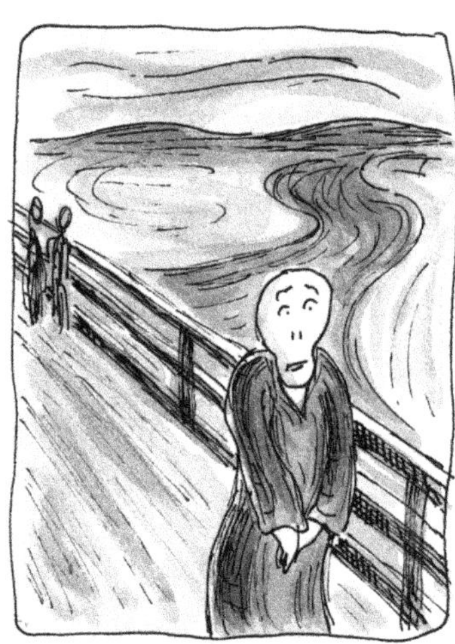

THE SIGH

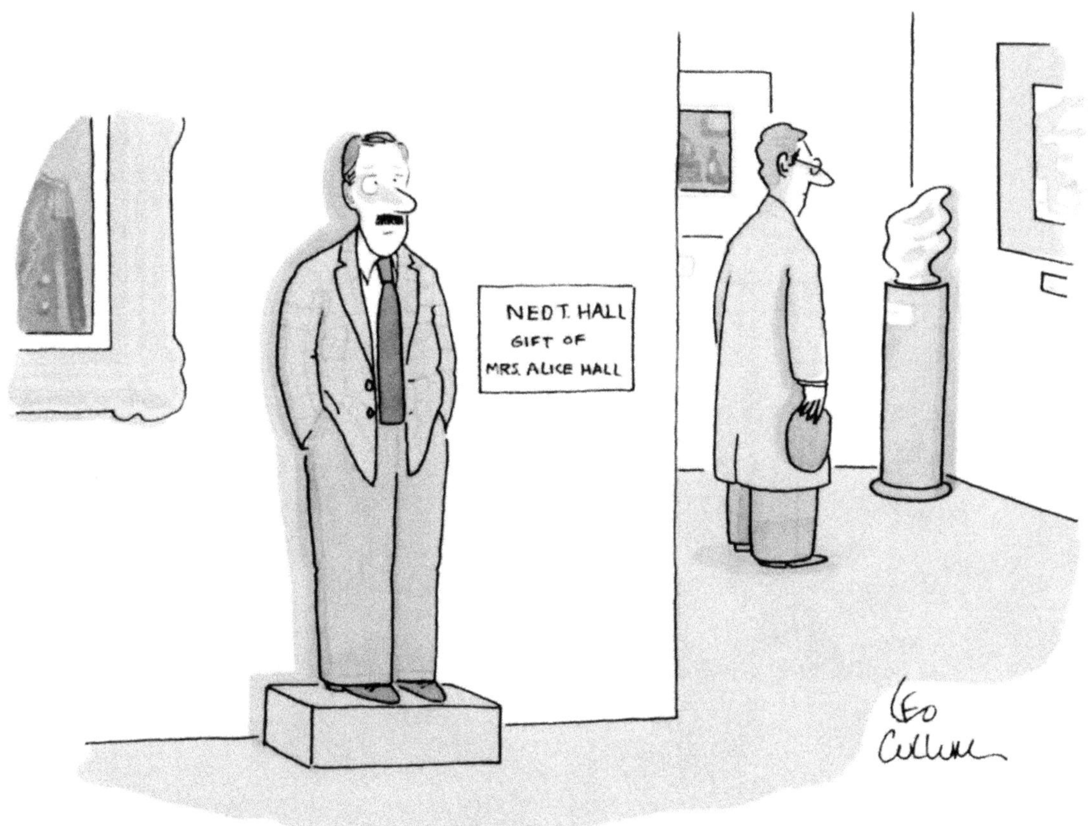
NED T. HALL
GIFT OF
MRS. ALICE HALL

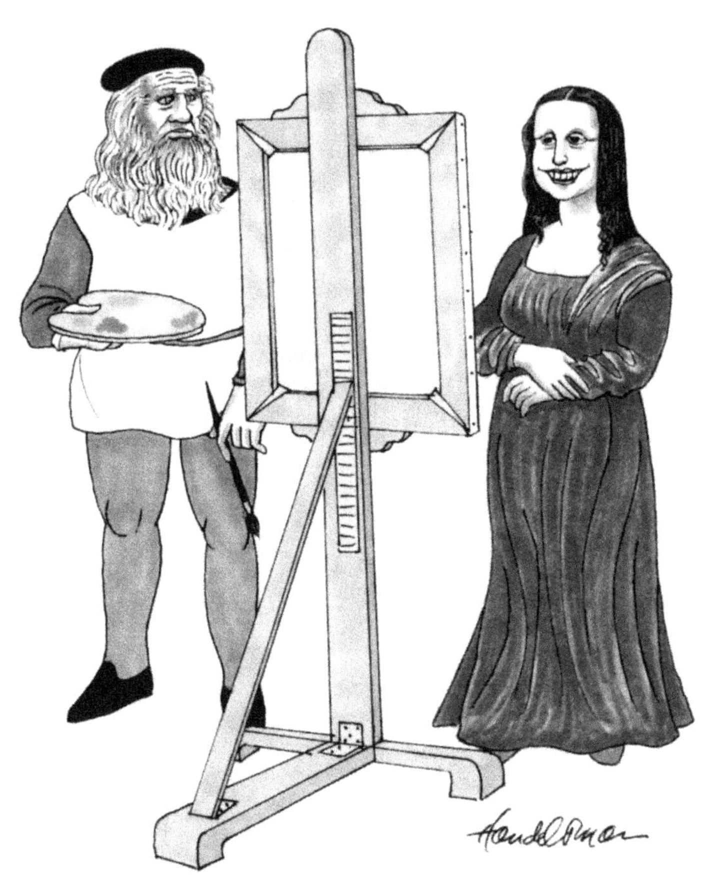

"It's nice, but I never smile like that. I smile like this."

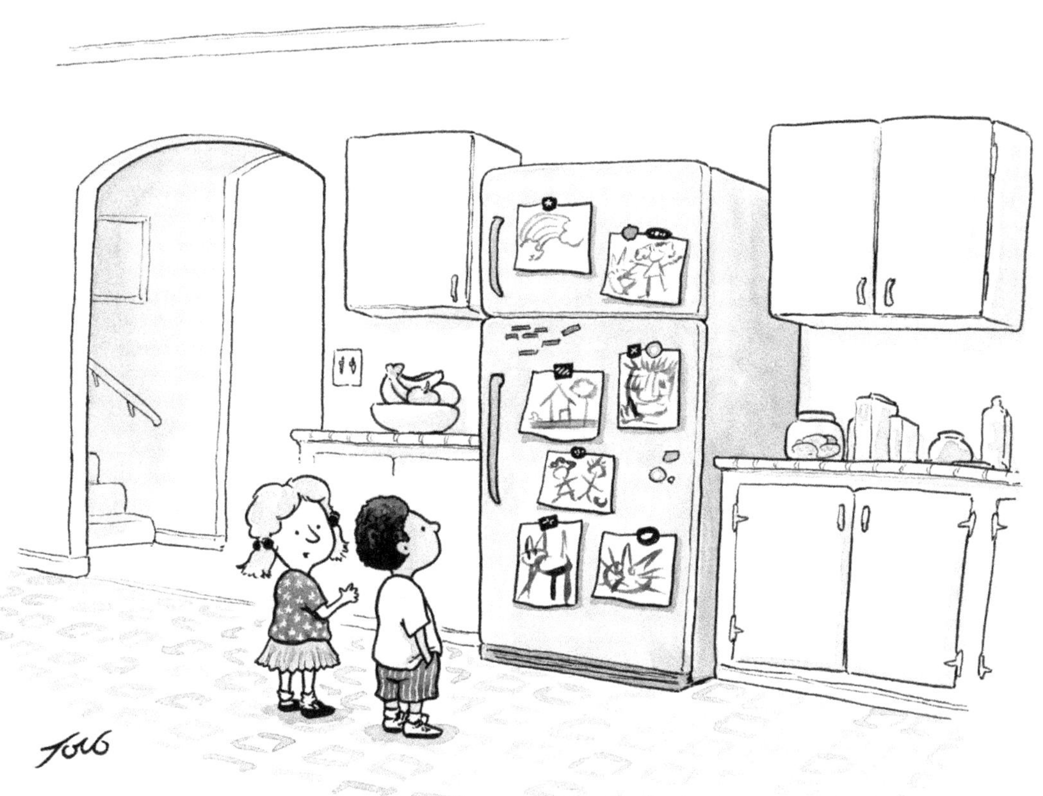

"I approach my subjects with an almost childlike sense of wonder."

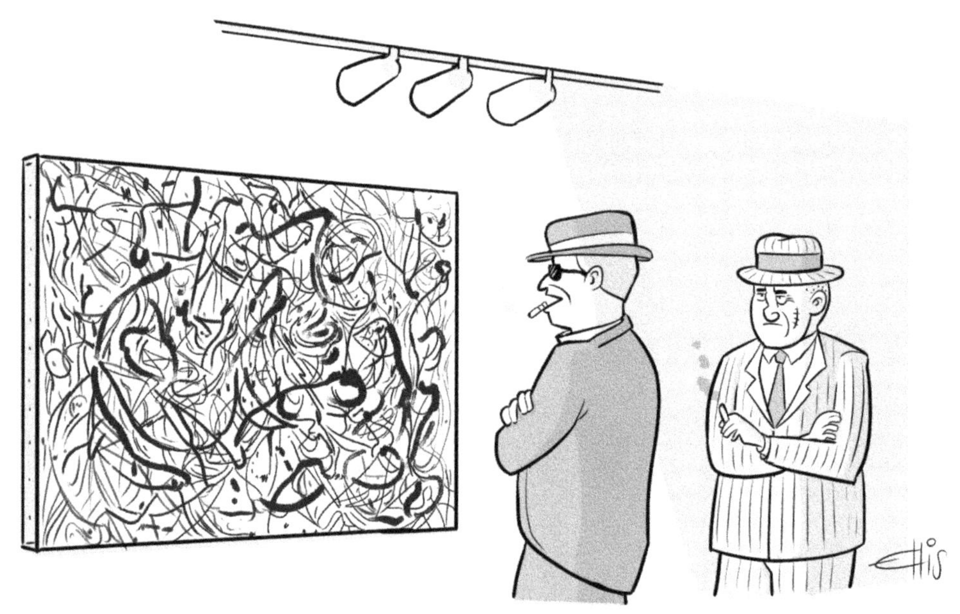

*"I like his style.
He makes it look like an accident."*

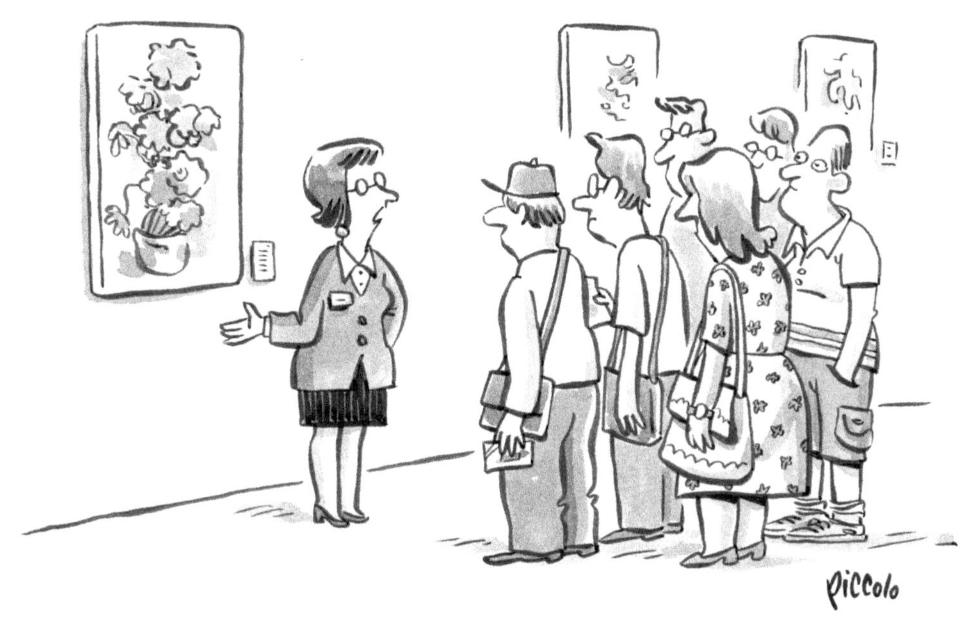

"Van Gogh would not live to see his masterpiece on a four-piece salad server set available in our gift shop."

Index of Artists

www.ingramcontent.com/pod-product-compliance
Lightning Source LLC
LaVergne TN
LVHW060602110826
845154LV00003B/19

9781963079081